D0793864

THE ANGEL'S DICTIONARY

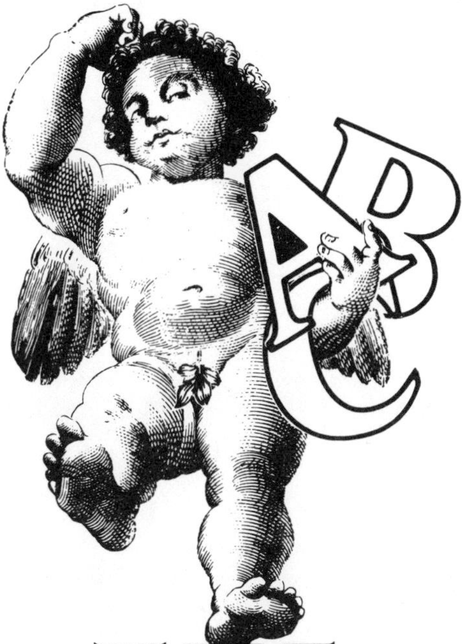

THE Angel's DICTIONARY

A MODERN TRIBUTE TO AMBROSE BIERCE

By

EDMUND H. VOLKART

Franklin Watts New York Toronto 1986

Library of Congress Cataloging-in-Publication Data

Volkart, Edmund Howell, 1919–
The angel's dictionary.

1. American wit and humor. I. Title.
PN6162.V58 1986 818′.5402 86-13292
ISBN 0-531-15001-1

Printed in the United States of America
6 5 4 3 2 1

I am profoundly grateful to Harry and Benna Lou Ball, and to Clark and Anne Connellee, for years of friendship above and beyond the usual call; to Ellen Joseph, editor extraordinary, for her keen eye and sharp pencil; and to Gerry McCauley for getting the entire project on track and keeping it there.

EHV

This book is seriously, and cheerfully, dedicated to Mother and Dad, who would have been amused; to Persh and Mary, and Kenneth and Shirley, who shared the laughter and the tears; to Karen and Kirsten, who taught us the joys of parenthood; and especially to Mary Ellen, who, for so many years, has held the pieces together with grace, humor, and compassion. She also promised not to laugh when I sat down to write and has kept that promise with charm and dignity.

EHV

THE ANGEL'S DICTIONARY

For anyone unacquainted with the delightful mysteries of Ambrose Bierce and *The Devil's Dictionary,* the title, subtitle, and text of this book will require a short explanation. The present title is intended to be a congenial counterpart to the original, retaining the same general theology. The subtitle signifies an intellectual debt to Bierce as well as my belief that his fiery spirit should be preserved in our time. The text is my attempt to vindicate this judgment.

Ambrose Gwinett Bierce was born in 1842, in Chester, Ohio, the youngest child of a large family. Unhappy with its pietistic stresses, he ran away from home at the age of fifteen. After several years of aimless drifting, he enlisted in the Union Army at the beginning of the Civil War. During the war he was seriously wounded and promoted to major for battlefield valor. A marriage in 1871 produced three children but a generally dismal family life. The date, location, and circumstances of his demise are unknown because he simply disappeared in 1913, presumably to join Pancho Villa's army in Mexico. What, at the age of seventy-one, he expected to accomplish there is known only to Bierce.

Such are the bare bones of Bierce's life, which can be said

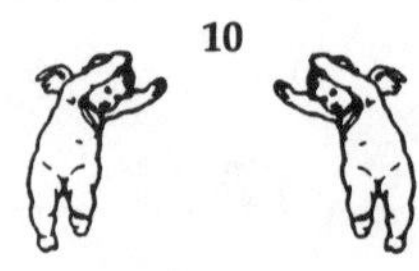

to have begun in misery and ended in mystery. In between, he had a colorful and controversial career.

Bierce compensated for his lack of formal education by developing keen powers of observation, a taste for wide reading, and a crisp, direct style of writing. In the decades after the Civil War he established himself as a very successful journalist and editor in the San Francisco area. He wrote short stories of considerable literary merit. Many of these still appear in anthologies or new collections issued both by commercial publishers and university presses. Much of this fiction seems derived from his response to family life, both in his early years and in marriage, and from his military experiences in the war. They provided him with a sardonic view of the world and its human inhabitants, embellished by a vivid imagination and a Poe-like preoccupation with horror and death.

Certainly, Bierce was a man of diverse talents, at least partially touched by genius, or madness, or both. Eccentric, irascible, and iconoclastic, he evoked strong reactions, positive or negative. His collected writings, including fiction, sketches, poems, satirical fables, and essays constitute a very respectable body of work totaling, in one edition, twelve substantial volumes. He has been the subject of numerous biographical and critical studies which, while scarcely unanimous in judgment or conclusion, firmly establish his reputation as a leading man of letters.

Yet it remains likely that the work for which Bierce is, and will be, best remembered is *The Devil's Dictionary,* which itself has an interesting history. He did not, like Samuel Johnson or Noah Webster, consciously and systematically set out to produce a Dictionary, satirical or otherwise. Beginning in 1881 in a weekly newspaper and continuing "in a desultory way and at long intervals," he published a series of definitions of common words and phrases, but endowed them with uncommon meanings. His ironic wit turned the conventional vocabulary upside down and inside out. This part of his literary output attracted considerable attention, if not notoriety, and humorists of the day were known to use his material often without attribution.

In 1906, many of these scattered lexicographical gems were collected and published as *The Cynic's Word Book,* a title, Bierce wrote, he "had not the power to reject nor the happiness to approve." In 1911, this time with the author's consent, the volume was reissued as *The Devil's Dictionary.*

For many entries in the *Dictionary,* a single sentence or phrase was sufficient to make the point; but often the basic definitions were accompanied by illustrative anecdotes, brief essays, or droll verses. Not a few of these were attributed to authors whose names derived from Bierce's comic imagination: Arbeley C. Strunk, Jex Wopley, Bogel S. Purvey, Oogum Bem, Bootle P. Gish, Joel Spate Woop, and similar worthies. Surely, W. C. Fields learned from Bierce in creating his own screen credits and names.

But it pleased Bierce to give explicit acknowledgment and recognition to "that learned and ingenious cleric, Father Gassalasca Jape, S. J." whose name and identity provide a clue to the intent and meaning of the book: to make a joke at the expense of the sacred. And, in this context, the "sacred" is not merely organized religion in general, or Catholicism in particular, but all that is deemed proper and worthy, fashionable and orthodox, learned and authoritative. As the title itself suggests, the book is meant to be "devilish," which is understandable from an author whose earlier (1872) book of satirical fables was called *The Fiend's Delight.*

In his Preface to the 1911 edition of *The Devil's Dictionary,* Bierce wrote that it was addressed to those "enlightened souls who prefer dry wine to sweet, sense to sentiment, wit to humor, and clean English to slang." But by almost any standard, the statement is far too modest for the text itself, an elegant understatement of all that it contains.

Indeed, the range and variety of the *Dictionary*'s entries, and the manner of their treatment, consistently elude adequate summary. Witness the following examples, selected for their brevity and scope:

> ADMIRATION, *n.* Our polite recognition of another's resemblance to ourselves.

ARISTOCRACY, *n.* Government by the best men. (In this sense the word is obsolete; so is that kind of government.)

CHRISTIAN, *n.* One who believes that the New Testament is a divinely inspired book admirably suited to the spiritual needs of his neighbor. One who follows the teachings of Christ in so far as they are not inconsistent with a life of sin.

CONSERVATIVE, *n.* A statesman who is enamored of existing evils, as distinguished from the Liberal, who wishes to replace them with others.

EDUCATION, *n.* That which discloses to the wise and disguises from the foolish their lack of understanding.

LAWYER, *n.* One skilled in circumvention of the law.

MARRIAGE, *n.* The state or condition of a community consisting of a master, a mistress and two slaves, making in all, two.

RADICALISM, *n.* The conservatism of tomorrow injected into the affairs of today.

SAINT, *n.* A dead sinner revised and edited.

UNDERSTANDING, *n.* A cerebral secretion that enables one having it to know a house from a horse by the roof on the house. Its nature and laws have been exhaustively expounded by Locke, who rode a house, and Kant, who lived in a horse.

There is dry wine here, but also acid; there is wit, but also wrath; there is sense, but also caustic satire. Clean English, not slang, does indeed prevail, but the economy of his style cannot conceal the richness of his thought. He had observed much, reflected deeply, and recorded his dissent.

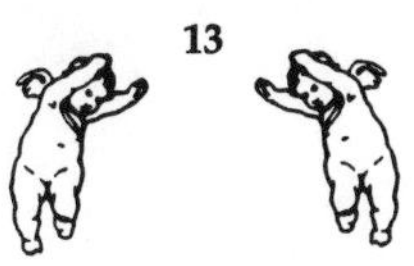

Fundamentally, I think, Bierce took a dim view of human nature and the institutions it had produced. He was particularly irritated by the apparent tendency of his fellows to uplift the trivial and dignify the commonplace. His mind was saturated with scepticism, making it an ideal instrument for the detection and dissection of the follies that surrounded him. Though he was often merely playful or gently ironic, he was also capable of looking upon a wicked world with mockingly wicked eyes.

Part of Bierce's short essay on "Satire" is worth quoting:

> In this country satire never had more than a sickly and uncertain existence, for the soul of it is wit, wherein we are dolefully deficient, the humor that we mistake it for, like all humor, being tolerant and sympathetic. Moreover, although Americans are "endowed by their Creator" with abundant vice and folly, it is not generally known that these are reprehensible qualities, wherefore the satirist is popularly regarded as a sour-spirited knave, and his every victim's outcry for codefendants evokes a national assent.

So it was that Bierce preferred the sting of satire to "tolerant and sympathetic" humor, and was prepared to receive the inevitable censure. It was well within his character, therefore, to define "Nonsense," as "the objections that are urged against this excellent dictionary."

In retrospect, it seems plain that the format of a dictionary was almost the perfect vehicle for Bierce's purposes. Many more targets could be covered more briefly than was possible, for example, with the essay form. Having examined the human condition and found it wanting in so many respects, he needed an appropriate means of expressing his disdain. If the world was indeed a stage, populated by vain, foolish, but pretentious actors, what better way to reveal its absurdities than by using the language of the script itself? In striking at conventional meanings, as embodied in the ordinary language, Bierce approached at least a level and

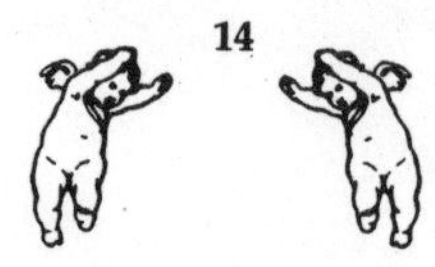

scope of satirical triumph that could be found only in the works of Juvenal, Swift, Voltaire, or La Rouchefoucald before him. Among American writers he belongs on the same shelf as Twain and Mencken.

It is important, I think, to understand that beneath the obvious witty surface of scorn and ridicule, the *Dictionary* was intended to be a serious work, worthy of serious attention. Relentlessly—some would say too relentlessly—Bierce was trying to tell us something about ourselves and the world we had created.

Yet despite this strong undercurrent of grim comment, *The Devil's Dictionary* is a funny book; it is a pleasure to read. Thus it has been discovered and rediscovered by successive generations, spurred on perhaps by H. L. Mencken's tribute that it contains "some of the most gorgeous witticisms in the English language."

However, there have been profound changes in the world since that time, more than a century ago, when Bierce began his weekly jibes. Of course, some elements of human folly are timeless and unchanging, but new ones are constantly being added. The very nature of the spheres of the sacred and the profane has been altered, and the script of the mad, modern, human comedy reads differently today. One wonders, for example, what Bierce would have made of nuclear arms, television and other marvels of mass communication, computers, the welfare state and its politics, the United Nations, the so-called sexual revolution, and countless other phenomena of our time and place in history.

All of which brings us to *The Angel's Dictionary*. I thought it would be challenging to try to update and expand upon that creative opening Bierce provided, to use a contemporary vocabulary to cast an amused, sceptical eye on our grave new world. Mainly, but not exclusively, *The Angel's Dictionary* is intended to be an exercise in satire, meaning that it will both offend and please people, even perhaps at the same time. And though ours is undoubtedly a wicked and dangerous world, it is not required that we be constantly grim and grave. So the book should also be read just for fun.

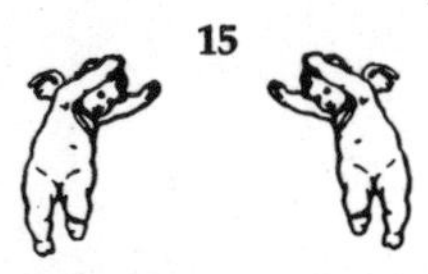

Few persons, and certainly not the present writer, can hope to approach or match the clean prose and pointed wit that marked Bierce's genius. *The Angel's Dictionary*, then, should be regarded as an imperfect attempt to do for our generation what Bierce did for his: to deplore the deplorable and to laugh at the laughable.

ABERRANT, *adj.* A hypercritical term applied by some people, who are envious, to other people, who are different.

ABET, *v.* To aid in a crime, as when a person places one where it is illegal to do so.

ABORTION, *n.* An issue of private morality that has become a public nuisance at the immoral hands of politics and the law.

ABSENCE, *n.* Lack of, as in, "Professors are notorious for the absence of presence of mind."

ABSTINENCE, *n.* That which makes the heart grow fonder for what is being abstained from; a virtue if practiced in moderation and silence.

ABSURD, *adj.* Unusually preposterous, such as grown men (or women) seriously debating how many nuclear warheads are dancing on the edge of World War III.

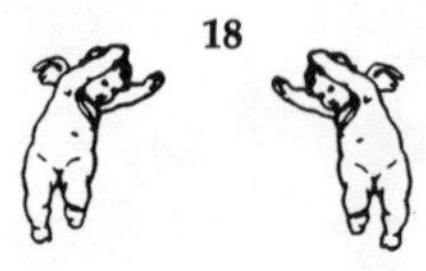

The world is our theater,
The play is quite absurd,
As statesmen seek their treaties
And ponder every word.
Acts One and Two are written,
Their lessons plain to see;
Now the savants quibble
Over lines for last Act Three.
They fiddle with the script,
While the only thing uncertain
Is who will be around
To pull the final curtain.

ORRY GLEIGER

ACADEMY, *n.* 1. Historically, a place of higher learning. In that sense, the word is obsolete; so is that kind of learning. 2. Currently known as Academia, it suffers from intellectual anemia, being inhabited by Schools of Education and Business Administration; assorted instant Institutes to study current fads; textbook writers; entrepreneurs of grantsmanship; political consultants of every known breed; Deans, Chancellors, Vice Presidents, and superfluous administrators of all stripes; and more committees than the number of students and faculty combined. It is a place where the sporting life wins, and the life of the mind loses.

ACCENT, *n.* The odd way other people talk; tolerable when natural, intolerable when faked.

ACCEPTED, *adj.* The prevailing level of stupidity, including the understanding that any other level of the same will be equally acceptable in the future.

ACCLIVITY, *n.* An upward slope, the downward of which is some disastrous proclivity.

ACCOUNTANT, *n.* A bookkeeper, or librarian of the loot, hired by everyone who needs defense against the IRS; must often display prowess as a juggler. A Certified Public Accountant is one trained and chartered to audit books or prepare financial statements according to the generally accepted rules of cheating.

ACHILLES HEEL, *n.* A fatal, well-concealed weakness of body or mind, usually the latter. (Slang: a Greek cad.)

ACQUAINTANCE, *n.* The status of another person whose degree of threat you are trying to determine. A nodding acquaintance is one in whose presence you can safely sleep.

ACTUARY, *n.* A statistically minded person who deals in numbers only, regardless of their numbing consequences for real people.

ADJUDICATION, *n.* A legal game in which courts try to find where legislatures have hidden justice.

ADOLESCENCE, *n.* A tiresome period of transition between childhood and adulthood, bearing the pain of both and the joy of neither.

ADULT EDUCATION, *n.* 1. A belated effort to correct the deficiencies of youthful education. 2. A meretricious scheme foisted upon middle-aged people with nothing better to do, by educators, do-gooders, and quacks of all kinds out to make a buck; a case of "Too little, too late."

"It is my fate to educate,"
Said the gray and kindly Dean;
"But I know at some late date
That learning leaves the scene.
Still, there's money there,
Like cotton candy at a Fair,
So when they bring their empty plate
I'll just pretend
Some food for thought is really there."

JASPER BRICKLEY

20

Achilles Heel

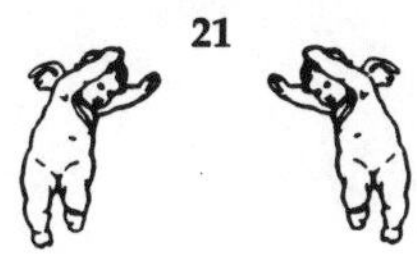

ADULTERY, *n.* An increasingly popular marital game, played out-of-bounds by at least one spouse, and preferably out of sight of officials or audience.

ADULT WESTERN, *n.* A new type of motion picture in which the cowboy hero is romantically torn between horse, heroin, and heroine.

ADVERTISEMENT, *n.* Formerly, a word meaning "information"; now, a synonym for heavily capitalized DECEIT, DECEPTION, and DISHONESTY.

ADVICE, *n.* A recommendation one makes at great peril, unless it's to oneself; even then it is suspect.

ADVOCATE, *n.* A person who pleads the cause of another. It is noteworthy that while almost anyone can play Devil's advocate, only a few are on the side of the Angels.

AESTHETE, *n.* A forlorn, arty person who professes to worship beauty, but never seems to find the right church.

AFFECTATION, *n.* A pretense, or artifice, such as professing to enjoy chamber music or liking George Steinbrenner.

AFFIDAVIT, *n.* A legal document for which an attorney or a notary public is paid to acknowledge that the lies made under oath are true.

AFFLUENCE, *n.* That opulent state of a nation's (or individual's) economy which precedes and precipitates total demoralization.

AFFRAY, *n.* A noisy brawl, which a prudent person is well advised to be afraid of.

AFORETHOUGHT, *adj.* Premeditated, as in "malice aforethought"; many afterthoughts have the same effect.

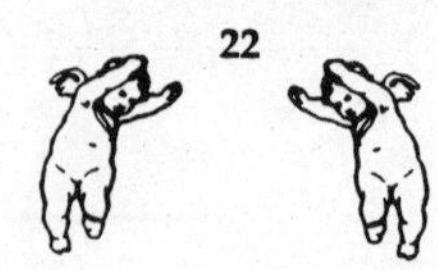

AFTEREFFECT, *n.* The same as a side effect, except that it comes later.

AGENT, *n.* Usually, a lowly person who is willing to lie or spy for anyone, so long as the price is right. The principal exception is the FBI agent, who is mysteriously endowed with matchless qualities of honor, courage, loyalty, truth, and omniscience.

AGE OF REASON, *n.* One never attained in history or life.

AGGRESSOR, *n.* A handy epithet applicable to any person or nation you want to fight anyway.

AGITATOR, *n.* A despicable person whom you secretly fear may be right.

AGNOSTIC, *n.* An honest person who admits he doesn't know; very, very rare.

What is so truly rare
As a genuine agnostic?
Only a learned Polar Bear
Who completes a double-crostic.

ODDLY J. DOLTER

AIR AGE, *n.* An actual historical period, now vanished forever, when people could breathe and enjoy it.

AIR BAG, *n.* A Congressman who inflates automatically whenever threatened by calamity. One of the most inspiring headlines in recent history read: "Congress approves air bags." What else is new?

ALARMIST, *n.* An excitable fellow who, anticipating the worst, can find it anywhere—even in good news.

ALCOHOL, *n.* A peculiar beverage, the use of which is variously denounced as sin, sickness, or crime (or all of the

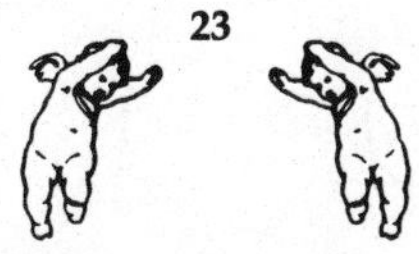

above)—regardless of proof. Fairness requires that this good book record the fact that many creative people in all walks of life have been admitted to the AlcoHol of Fame.

ALLEGIANCE, *n.* What one pledges to flag and country in the absence of anything more substantial.

ALL FOOL'S DAY, *n.* The one after every fool's night; recognized by multitudes every day of the year with more remorse than gratitude.

ALLIES, *n. pl.* 1. Those people on *our* side, we believe, as opposed to the ones on *their* side, who are dupes, captives, pawns, satellites, etc., etc. 2. Yesterday's enemies who have profited so much in defeat that they are happy to let buygones be buygones. 3. Tomorrow's enemies.

ALTRUISM, *n.* Not a truism at all, but a falsism by means of which cunning selfishness is disguised as noble motive.

ALUMNUS, *n.* A graduate of a particular college or university, who is incessantly reminded of the fact by endless fund raising drives. Just why anyone who managed to escape from the Alma Mater with a reasonable degree of sanity should be so hounded is one of the mysteries of higher education.

AMATEUR, *n.* A person who behaves like a professional, and often better, but who lacks the latter's prestige and prosperity.

AMBITION, *n.* A strong, respectable desire for success, fame, or honor; better described as unsightly than blind. It is particularly admired among the incompetent as a symbol of virtue.

AMEND, *v.* To rewrite a law in such a way as to further obscure its already confused meaning.

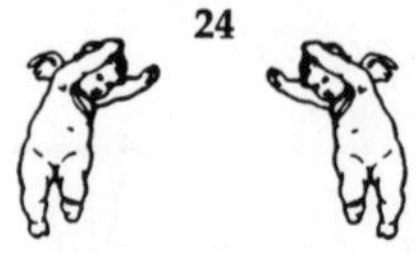

AMENDMENT, *n.* The logical product of the amending process that serves chiefly as a make-work program for lawyers, and a new arena for judicial tyranny.

AMERICAN PLAN, *n.* An integral part of foreign policy under which armaments are sold impartially to friends, enemies, friends of enemies, and enemies of friends. After the inevitable wars ensue, the same policy requires foreign aid be provided. Sometimes referred to as *Pox Americana.*

ANATOMY, *n.* Formerly, a contact sport usually played by two people at a time in private; now, any number of any sex can play it any time, anywhere, at any rate.

"Anatomy is destiny,"
Wrote Dr. Sigmund Freud,
By which he seemed to mean
A fate we can't avoid
As long as sexual differences
Are properly employed.
But this is now disputed
On one specific ground:
A sexual orientation
Ought never be pronouned.
What difference does it make
If it's he, she, or them?
Let's not argue gender
Much less ad hominem.

ORVILLE SMUTSCH

ANCIENT HISTORY, *n.* Last week's gossip, and yesterday's news.

ANGEL, *n.* A cherubic denizen of heaven that beatifically lent its good name to this saintly dictionary.

ANTI-CLERICAL, *adj.* Formerly, a popular attitude of opposition toward petty, tyrannical priests; now, and more justly, directed against petty, tyrannical government clerks who have outdone the priests.

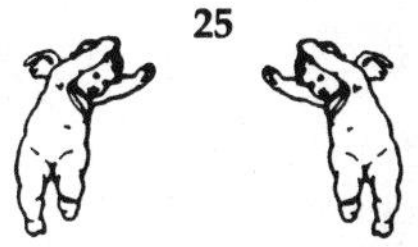

ANTIHERO, *n.* A popular protagonist in the modern novel who, being antagonistic toward all things worthy, is clearly worth being written and read about.

ANTIPERSPIRANT, *n.* A chemical substance that subsidizes all those armpits on television.

APATHY, *n.* Indifference or unconcern. It is said to cause the general lack of participation in the American political process—another case of the effect being confused with cause.

APPELLATE COURT, *n.* One whose principal function is to find narrow, technical reasons for miscarriages of justice.

APPRAISAL, *n.* An evaluation, which is always high for property taxes, and always low for property losses.

APTITUDE TEST, *n.* A modern device purporting to discover what skills and talents a person has, to better prepare for the proper career. Extensive research reveals that the most important aptitude is the one for taking and passing tests.

AQUA PURA, *n.* Pure water; now, both extinct and obsolete.

ARABIAN NIGHTS, *n.* Those desperate periods of darkness following upon dazzling Israeli days.

ARCHBISHOP, *n.* A high church official now swallowing a bitter pill.

Said one Archbishop to the others,
"Now that the flock can have its druthers,
I think our rhythm's lost its beat
And Papal Bull its holy heat;
The Church's word they do not hear
But to the Pill they will adhere."

MICKEY SLECTER

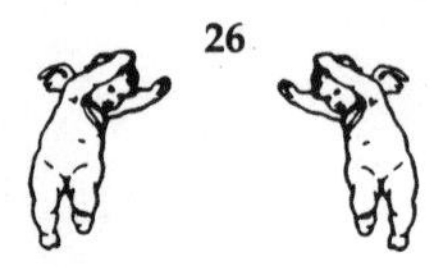

ARISTOCRAT, *n.* A worthless member of the hereditary upper classes of Europe, highly esteemed by the democratic American middle class.

ARMPIT, *n.* An unsightly part of the human anatomy, thoughtfully covered by nature with a shoulder, but now triumphantly displayed in television commercials.

ARROGANCE, *n.* That trait of self-confident righteousness attributed to others by those who wish they possessed it.

ART, *n.* In modern usage any form of representation that studiously avoids the portrayal of the good, the true, and the beautiful.

ARTIFICIAL INSEMINATION, *n.* A scientific gift, frozen and then thawed to impregnate the infertile. ("Yes, Vagina, there is a Santa Claus.")

ASPIRATION, *n.* The goal one seeks, as distinguished from inspiration, which is needed for fulfillment. There seem to be many more aspirations than inspirations to go around.

ASSET, *n.* Anything that has value. Thus, in Hawaii, the famous hula dance is an asset to music and to spectators.

ATOMIC BOMB, *n.* A very large, lethal bomb which, when dropped, has the unfortunate tendency to atomize everything in the vicinity.

ATTORNEY GENERAL, *n.* The chief law enforcement officer of a government whose major task is to protect and defend that government in its illegal activities.

AUDITOR, *n.* A professional person paid to certify that the cheating of bookkeepers meets the standard level of competence.

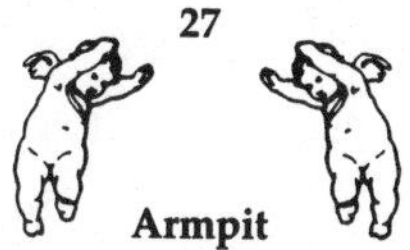

27

Armpit

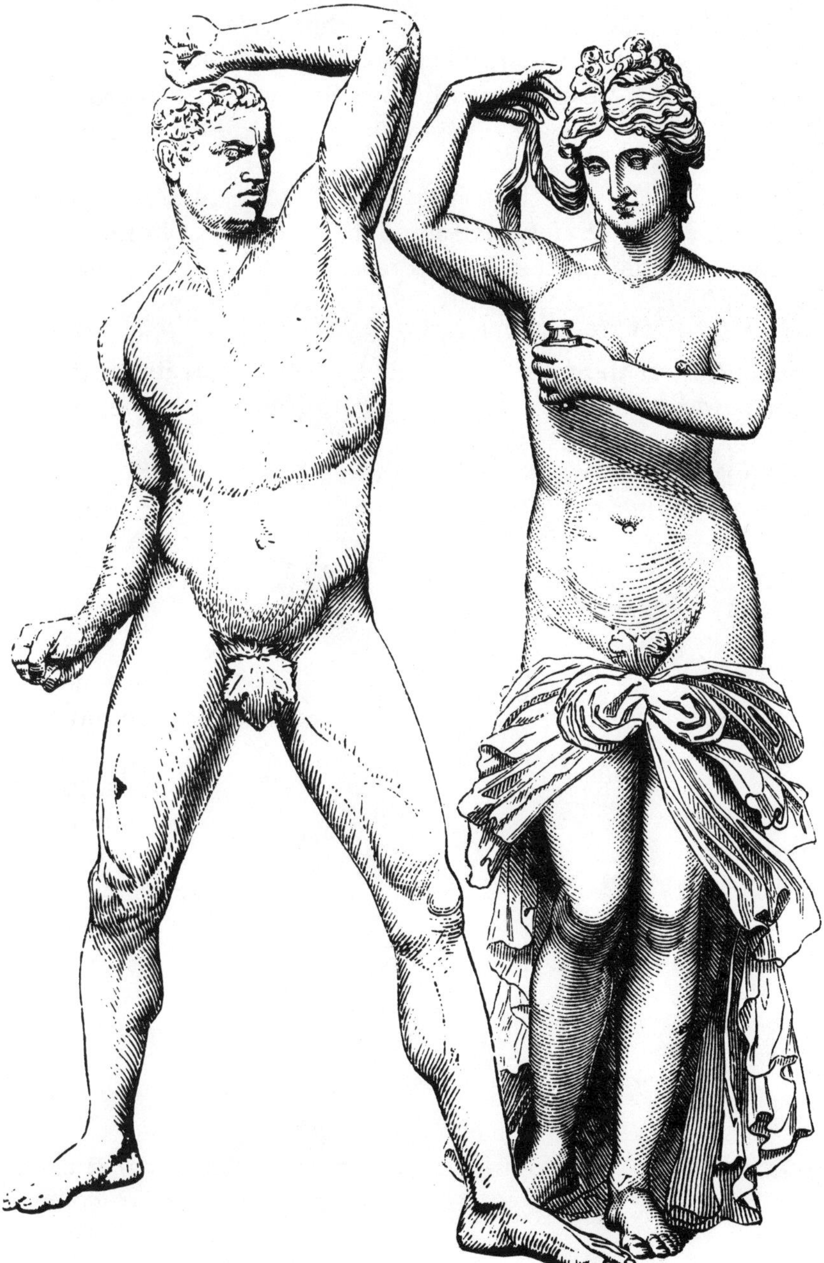

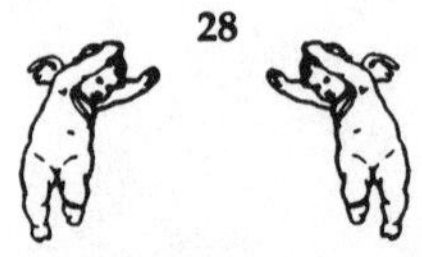

AUTOMATION, *n.* A much admired self-correcting technological system developed by man to control machines. Fortunately, despite many efforts, this system is still undeveloped, or out-of-order, when applied to people—except for the incidental result of adding to the ranks of the unemployed.

AUTONOMY, *n.* The highly prized state of self-government, or independent existence, that always seems to disappear just as it comes within reach.

AVANT GARDE, *n.* The Pied Pipers of new movements, especially in the arts, who cultivate and captivate the witless and the aimless, thereby receiving much attention.

AXIOMS, *n. pl.* Self-evident truths which, in all societies, far outnumber any other kind.

BABY, *n.* A precious little thing which many say is too often thrown out with the bath water; according to ecologists, futurists, and others of similar persuasion, this is perfectly proper if the water is recycled.

BABY GRAND, *n.* The first one; after that it's baby-sitter.

BACCALAUREATE, *n.* A ritualistic address delivered at commencement ceremonies for the benefit of the speaker—the only one listening.

BACHELOR, *n.* A man singularly successful in avoiding double jeopardy.

BACK, *n.* A part of the body that can bite when someone else's is turned.

BACTERIA, *n. pl.* The populous, non-paying patrons of a cafeteria.

BAIL, *n.* What is required by courts when a prisoner's word is not his bond, and his appearance is dubious.

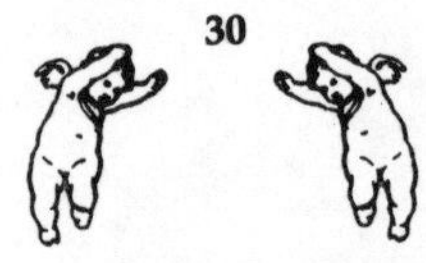

BAKER'S DOZEN, *n.* Traditionally, thirteen units instead of twelve; now, it is more likely to be eleven, and counting down.

BALANCE OF POWER, *n.* A time-tested doctrine of international diplomacy, whereby the military strength of all the major nations is so much in balance that no single nation will dare attack another—that is left to groups of allies. In this manner, world wars, instead of local conflicts, are assured.

BALLISTIC MISSILE, *n.* A long-range offensive weapon; very offensive at any range.

Superpowers for war have planned,
Missiles placed on sea and land,
While clocks display the fatal hand;
And should we wake before we die,
There won't be time to say "Goodbye,"
Just enough to weep and cry;
No parade, no marching band,
But by the blast we'll all be tanned,
What an ending, simply grand.

ELROY KRIMP

BALLOT, *n.* In democracies, the means by which the lesser of two or more political evils is transformed into the "people's choice."

BAN, *n.* An official prohibition, an outstanding example being Prohibition itself, which was a failure, as are most bans. It is in the nature of legislators to want to ban many more things than they permit, so long as they themselves are exempt. The phrase, "Against the law" is well known, but whoever heard of "For the law"?

BANKS, *n. pl.* Financial institutions that are respectable, but not without their failings.

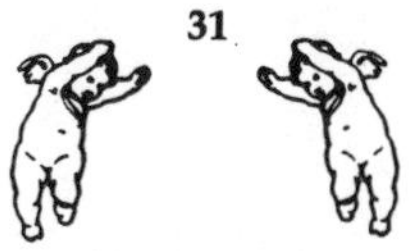

BAPTISM, *n.* A Christian rite in which innocent infants are purified in polluted water.

BARBARIAN, *n.* An uncivilized person, that is, anyone whose prejudices and practices differ from our own.

BARBAROUS, *adj.* Coarse or crude, such as Congressional hearings and wrestling matches which have in common meaningless grunts and much breast beating.

BARRACKS, *n.* An inhuman living arrangement in which the imperfections of each resident are revealed to all, to the betterment of none.

BARREN, *adj.* Without children; what would benefit everyone if more people were.

BARTENDER, *n.* A splendid person who practices psychiatry on the cheap by keeping his mouth closed, his ears open, and the glass filled.

BASKETBALL, *n.* A character-building sport in which deliberate fouling is a legitimate strategy, and the outcome of a contest often depends more on official calls than on player performance.

> When James was a lad, the sport called basketball was just becoming popular. He himself did not care for the game but, somewhat strangely, his mother became infatuated with it. Every year she would form a team to compete with other local teams, and winning became her sole ambition. Adroitly, she managed to have a close friend named as referee for most of the games. Foul after foul would be whistled against her opponents, while the sins of her own players were conveniently overlooked. With this official assistance, James's mother had many winning teams and became part of local folklore.

32

Bathing Beauty

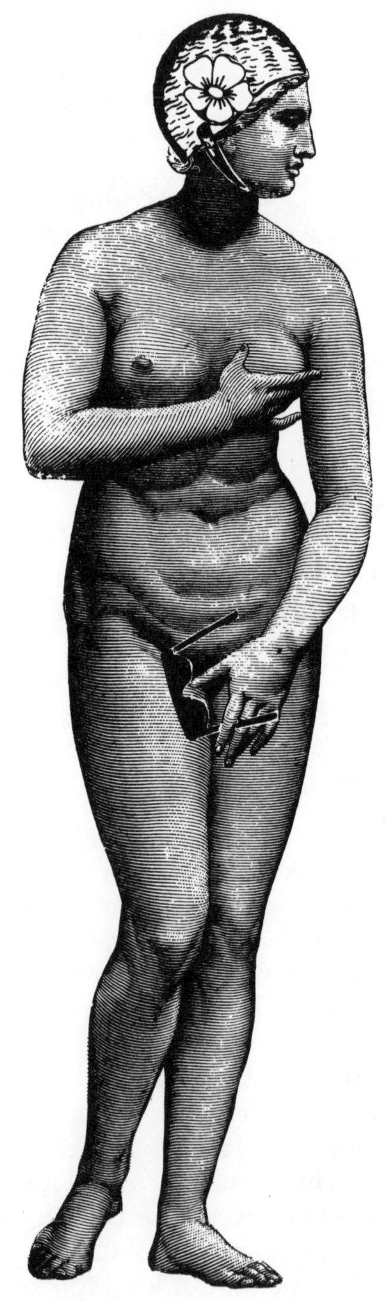

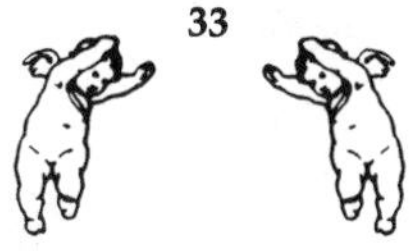

In the meantime, James had gone off to study and became an artist. Once, when he returned on a visit to his home town, he painted a picture of the notorious referee in his uniform. Its formal name was "An Arrangement in Gray and Black," but it is now best known as "Mother's Whistler."

ARBY TWENT

BATHING BEAUTY, *n.* A girl who enjoys the maximum of exposure with a minimum of enclosure.

BATTLE CRY, *n.* The anguished weeping of those involved in, or bereaved by war; a universally ignored sound.

BATTLE STATION, *n.* A dangerous depot on the track of combat where soldiers await the next strain.

BEAUTY SHOP, *n.* A place where women pay for new disguises.

BELEAGUER, *n.* To beset or harass; the way football and baseball fans feel when players go on strike.

BELIEF, *n.* An opinion or judgment; a word that should preface every purported statement of fact, but doesn't.

BELITTLE, *v.* To make seem small or unimpressive, which means that most public figures can never truthfully be belittled.

BENIGN, *adj.* In modern usage, a seemingly harmless form of neglect, which has the habit of becoming malicious.

BENIGHTED, *adj.* Ignorant, which is why so many people addressed as "Sir" in Great Britain are said to be knighted.

BIAS, *n.* Your prejudiced opinion, as opposed to my judicious one.

BIBLE BELT, *n.* A generous slug of theological brew which, when taken liberally and literally, produces hellishly holy heavens.

BICAMERAL, *adj.* Having two legislative bodies, which means twice as much damage can be done as with a unicameral one, which is one too many.

BIG, *adj.* Of great size; nearly always bad in condition and consequence. Consider bigots and bigamy. Then recall Orwell's Big Brother; James Joyce's comment, "I hate big words"; or Mr. Justice Brandeis remarking on the "curse of bigness"; or Hitler's demonic use of "The Big Lie." The great American doctrine that "bigger is better" has little support, except perhaps from elephants.

BIGAMIST, *n.* A marital masochist.

BIOGRAPHY, *n.* The life story of a person as written by a novelist, especially if it's authorized.

BIOLOGICAL WARFARE, *n.* As a gentle war between the sexes, it is fun; as a part of military might, it is deadly serious.

BIORHYTHM, *n.* The official Catholic method of birth control, if one is prepared to face the music.

BIRTHDAY, *n.* An annual reminder that the more you slow down, the more time accelerates.

BLAMEWORTHY, *adj.* Deserving to be blamed; not to be confused with unworthy which means only undeserving.

BLANK VERSE, *n.* Poetry written without rhyme, often without reason.

BLASPHEMY, *n.* The profane abuse of sacred things, as found in choir practice and church suppers.

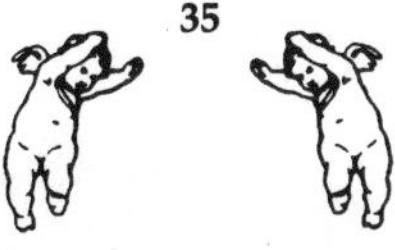

BLESSED EVENT, *n.* A questionably sacred designation for a rather secular happening.

BLOCKBUSTER, *n.* A literary best seller that has passed the weight test, the thickness test, and the title test—all the tests but quality control.

BLOOD RELATIVE, *n.* A person related by birth if there's good blood; by marriage if bad.

BLUE LAWS, *n. pl.* The silly ones, such as prohibiting the sale of various items on Sunday. Fortunately, they are becoming obsolete, amended by the green laws of money.

BLUNDERBUSS, *n.* An awkward kiss, but capable of leading to more serious blunders such as matrimony and children.

BOAR, *n.* A wild pig, usually sitting next to you at a dinner party.

BODY LANGUAGE, *n.* A form of expression that requires no words. In subdued usage it is found among silent movie comedians, golfers, and people who play pin-ball machines. More explicit practitioners were Salome, Gypsy Rose Lee, Mae West, and Elvis Presley. A dictionary is not needed.

BOMBAST, *n.* A type of speech, usually political, featuring a surplus of words and a deficit of meaning.

BONDAGE, *n.* The state or condition a person finds himself in after reading too many novels by Ian Fleming.

BONE OF CONTENTION, *n.* A brief history of paleontology.

BORDER, *n.* A more or less clearly defined line separating two populations smart enough to mistrust each other. When it is relatively unguarded, there is only the normal amount

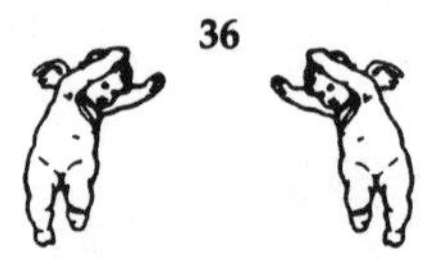

of suspicion; when heavily fortified, trouble is ahead and tourists are advised to stay home.

BORN-AGAIN CHRISTIAN, *n.* A person who missed the gospel singers the first time around, and now announces he has joined the choir.

BOTANY, *n.* The science of plants, as in "The FBI and the CIA practice botany by means of wiretaps, bugs, etc."

BOTTOM LINE, *n.* The one that businessmen and politicians advise us to look at while they manipulate the top lines that produce it.

BOURBON, *n.* The tasty ingredient which, along with scotch, makes polluted water potable.

BOURGEOISIE, *n.* The middle class, so called because it is caught between high taxes and low esteem.

BRAGGART, *n.* An insufferable person who talks more about himself than about you; when you do the same, you are being sociable.

BRAIN, *n.* The engine of the mind, usually with a few missing spark plugs.

BRAIN DRAIN, *n.* The result of the process of deep thinking, which suggests it is not a serious problem.

BRAIN TRUST, *n.* An unofficial group of advisers who have gained the trust of an officeholder, and earned the distrust of everyone else.

BRAINWASHING, *n.* A dubious, modern educational technique suspected of changing bad habits and cleaning dirty minds.

BRAND NAME, *n.* The one by which a particular product

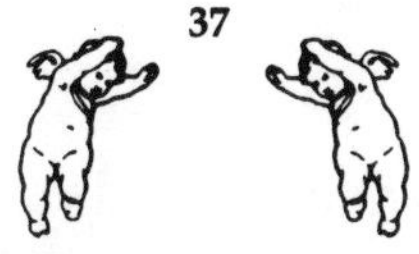

or commodity is best known, even if its advertising almost always claims it is brand new.

BRAZIER, *n.* A metal container to hold burning coals, or a person who works in brass; neither should be confused with a feminine garment in a spelling match or anywhere else.

BREAK DANCING, *n.* A recent, popular terpsichorean invitation to visit a chiropractor.

BREATHLESS, *adj.* What a good, breath-taking vodka will leave you.

BREVITY, *n.* The soul of wit and the goal of women's wear.

BRIBE, *n.* An offer or a payment to someone to do something wrong or illegal, e.g., the budget of the CIA.

BRIDE, *n.* Formerly, an innocent woman (usually blushing) who accepted a ring and a vow in exchange for bed and board. Now, a woman of experience, incapable of blushing, but who has vowed to know a good ring when she sees one.

BRIDEGROOM, *n.* A man who has always known the difference between bed and bored, but is willing to offer a ring and a vow in the hope that the ease of bed will compensate for the boredom.

BRINKMANSHIP, *n.* A diplomatic way of playing "chicken," or Russian roulette.

BROAD-MINDED, *adj.* The liberal toleration of that which is unconventional or otherwise deplorable.

To be broad-minded is a virtue;
Narrow-minded a sin—
Which is very odd.
It's always been the straight and narrow

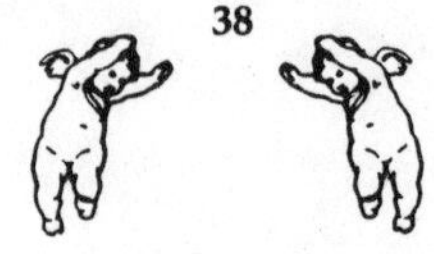

That led to God,
And broads that led to gin.

AMY PLIECE

BUCK, *n.* (slang) A dollar, or what passes for one; also what one passes to another in order to escape blame.

"The buck stops here,"
Was Harry Truman's vow;
And when he fired MacArthur
He stirred up quite a row.
The buck was worth more then
Than is the dollar now.

DRAB K. DRIMBLE

BUDGET, *n.* A financial plan that succeeds only if you fudge it.

BUFFOON, *n.* A rather awkward synonym for a clown. Imagine a song entitled, "Send in the Buffoons."

BUNCOMBE, *n.* Humbug or nonsense, which is why the United States Congress is often referred to as "The Battle of Buncombe Hill."

BUNGLE, *v.* To make something in an inferior or clumsy way; developers build bunglelows to be sold at a very high price.

BUREAUCRAT, *n.* A petty official who thinks he should be promoted because he has learned how to add glue to the already existing red tape.

BUSING, *n.* A judicially mandated, injudicious attempt to solve troublesome problems of discrimination in education by referring them to equally troublesome problems of transportation.

BUSYBODY, *n.* A popular prostitute.

CABLE TELEVISION, *n.* A splendid addition to ordinary television in that it increases the choices among entirely interchangeable programs.

CAESAR'S WIFE, *n.* A woman, usually the wife of a political leader, who must be above suspicion and not under indictment.

CALCULATED RISK, *n.* A military term used to justify a failed combat operation that was badly calculated in the first place.

CALISTHENICS, *n.* A ritual set of physical exercises engaged in, and enjoyed by, all the healthy people who don't need them.

CALL GIRL, *n.* One who receives more engagement than wedding rings, with no visible signs of regret, but many visible signs of support.

CAMELOT, *n.* A legendary place with round tables and square knights.

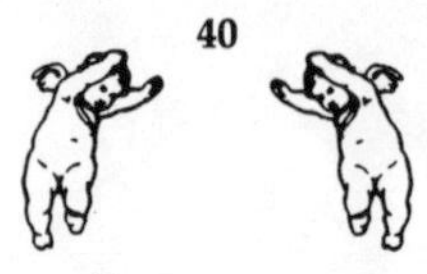

Queen Guinivere, severe was not,
Especially with Sir Lancelot,
Who came a lot
To Camelot,
Thus giving pain to Sir Gawain
And adding much to Arthur's strain
As the Court began to wane.

IGOR MINSTREL

CAMERA OBSCURA, *n.* The one used in making most modern films.

CANT, *n.* Insincere talk, the can-do of politicians and undertakers.

CAPITALISM, *n.* An economic system in which some people exploit other people, as distinguished from Communism where the reverse is true.

CAPITAL PUNISHMENT, *n.* In its most cruel form, this dreadful event occurs when a member of Congress learns he or she has been defeated for re-election.

CAREER GIRL, *n.* A person of the female gender who endures the humdrum drudgery of the workplace rather than the humdrum drudgery of the home, then boasts of her liberation.

CASE WORKER, *n.* In the social services, a person more likely to have a soft heart than a hard nose.

CASTANETS, *n. pl.* The clicking musical signal to begin fishing.

CAT, *n.* A small, furry, funny, four-legged domestic pet, the only species to ever completely master the art of studied indifference toward all other creatures, especially man; the sovereign of all beasts.

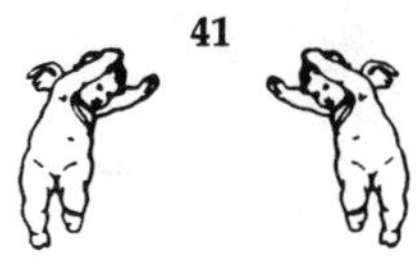

I think that I would like to be my cat.
Not any cat, you understand, but mine:
The gray one, with stripes in line
And lives that number more than nine.
He's not too short, not too tall,
Not too large, not too small,
Yet has more parts than all of Gall
And scorns the arts of protocol.

With solemn eyes that seem quite wise
He will arise with no surprise
And view the world without disguise;
No need to fawn or be a pawn,
Nor fake a smile to hide a yawn,
Or try to cross some Rubicon.
When he awakes to face the dawn
He looks across the verdant lawn
As if to find a Leprechaun—
And then to wish that he were gone
To sight some birds, or have some words,
With other cats about the night
And what to do in morning's light:
It might be fun to fly a kite
Or make a run that's out of sight,
If just to raise an appetite.

He comes and goes with every whim,
Each room for him becomes a gym
For rolling over, testing straws,
Or biting things with busy jaws—
A free-born rebel without laws
And no mystique of Santa Claws.
With hooded eyes he curls and lies
Awaiting his next exercise
Which, upon my own surmise,
Requires no time to catalyze:
He's not the one to analyze
Or contemplate his own demise,
Whate'er his fate, no alibis.

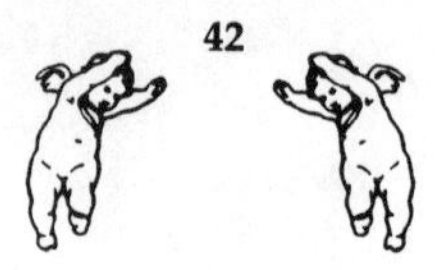

His way of life is full of charm,
Well-fed, well-tended, free from harm,
He has no cause to feel alarm
Or move to cities from the farm;
His world is one of no demands
And if he hears my few commands
He shuts his ears and struts away
To rub around some other day,
As if to say that he is fey
And I'm the one who's lost the way.

For every lock he holds the keys,
Feels no need to beg or please
And lives his life of feline ease.
He sees no lands to grasp or squeeze,
Pays no tax or parking fees:
They're man's, not cat's, disease.

If God begat a new format
I think I'd rather be my cat.
Men must form their own relations,
Set their norms for social stations
And pay allegiance to their nations.
But not my cat.
He's oblivious to all of that
(Indeed, I think he smells a rat).
He's not a fool or diplomat,
Pays no dues, wears no hat,
Hates no Jews or things like that.
He makes no case to save his face,
Invokes no race for special place,
And worries not about disgrace
Or who is first in outer space.

Perhaps from pools of feline genes
He needs no tools or slick machines,
Endless schools or benzedrines,
Commercial Yules or movie queens,
Deadly bombs or submarines;
No stones to throw, or taps to blow,
No grains to sow, or debts to owe,

He keeps his profile very low.
Inspired by flags and catechisms
Men create their many schisms
Seen through ethnocentric prisms;
But strange to say, in his quaint way,
My Tigger fears no Cataclysms.

So when I think of all of that—
The life of man, the life of cat—
I dare not add a caveat:
For when I go to where IT'S at
The King I see may be a cat!

FELINIUS O. MAGNUM

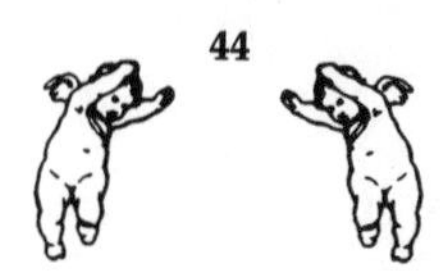

CATECHISM, *n.* For learning Christian doctrine, a book of questions and answers, in which the nature of the latter determines the form of the former.

CAVEAT EMPTOR, *n.* A Latin phrase meaning "The cave is empty," especially if purchased from a merchant who promised to furnish it.

CEASE-FIRE, *n.* A mutually agreed upon time-out in the game of war, brief enough to prevent peace but long enough to permit reinforcements. Protocol requires that each side claim violations by the other, both of whom are right.

CENSOR, *n.* An officious meddler who, believing that everyone else is as dangerous or depraved as he or she is, thinks that they must be protected against themselves.

CEPHALIC INDEX, *n.* A notoriously unreliable means used by women to estimate masculine virility.

CEREMONY, *n.* A formal ritual, inordinately lengthy, upon which a large amount of money is spent in a vain attempt to dignify a catastrophe about to happen.

CHARITY, *n.* A widely esteemed public display of generosity that disguises a guilty conscience.

CHASTITY, *n.* An old-fashioned virtue that has become a modern vice due to peer aversion.

Faith, Hope, and Chastity:
Of these mighty three,
The first two
Will have to do.

JADED SWIFT

CHAUVINIST, *n.* An unreasonable, warlike patriot who thinks, and says, that everyone else should be willing to die for *his* country.

CHECKMATE, *n.* The spouse who banks on holding the purse strings.

CHECKS AND BALANCES, *n.* A novel feature of American democracy that permits government checks to find their way into many bank balances.

CHILDHOOD, *n.* The happiest time of life because there isn't much to look back on with regret.

CHIP(S), *n. pl.* An under-rated word of such remarkable versatility as to defy definition; it can only be illustrated in bits and pieces. An aggressive person carries one on his shoulder; a son, but rarely a daughter, can be one off the old block; a diplomat seeks one to bargain with; a golfer uses it to get onto the green; an investor wants a blue one; and a computer whiz wants his in silicon.

Plurally speaking, if you're lucky in poker you can cash them in, but if you did that in the Old West you were dead; you can eat potato ones with your sandwich, or chocolate ones in your cookies; a reckless person will let them fall where they may, but may also cautiously hurl cow or buffalo chips in a contest. Finally, and curiously, you will know when the chips are down, but not when they're up.

CHRISTMAS, *n.* A season of the year requiring suspension of the normal state of selfishness. Fortunately, it is temporary and easily endured.

CHURCH, *n.* A religious building of such paramount significance that it is sometimes used more than one day a week.

CITIZEN, *n.* A stately word intended to relieve us of the burdensome thought that paying taxes is our primary duty.

CITY FATHERS, *n. pl.* The leaders of the community, so named because they treat everyone else as if they were naughty children.

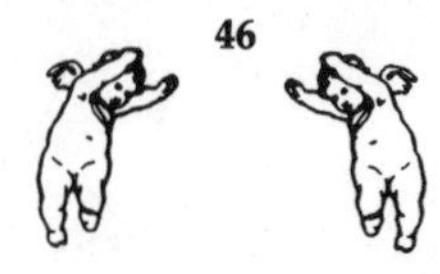

CITY PLANNING, *n.* An urban concept, practiced so diligently that most cities are utterly uninhabitable as well as ungovernable.

CIVIL DEFENSE, *n.* An elaborate form of public protection that is always late to work.

CIVILIZED, *adj.* Sane, urbane, refined, all the qualities that have been rejected by the modern world, and are barely surviving elsewhere.

CIVIL RIGHTS, *n. pl.* 1. The weak ones remaining after being punched by everyone else's uncivil lefts. 2. Legal powers sought by everyone, the better to commit uncivil wrongs.

CIVIL SERVANTS, *n. pl.* Honored employees of the public who have mastered the art of servile supremacy.

CLAQUE, *n.* A noisy clique.

CLASS, *n.* A category of people, with membership in one group precluding membership in another. In the beginning, there were two sub-species: those who had it and those who didn't. Marx saw this as a problem and proposed solving it with a classless society, thereby assuring that no one would have it. Recently, class concepts have exploded: the leisure class, the working class, the old class, the new class, the under class, the over class, the middle class, the upper class, the lower class, and world class. As the teacher used to say, "Class is over." Any noun that can have so many conflicting modifiers can't mean much, except to those interested in class conflict.

CLASS CONSCIOUSNESS, *n.* An idea popularized by Marx, fostering the dubious belief that divergent selves should have their consciousness raised to forge a mystical identity with the unidentifiable.

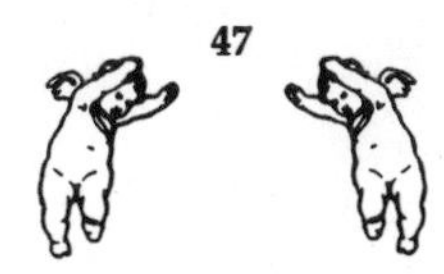

CLASSICAL, *adj.* A derisive form of praise applied to anything currently out of fashion, especially in art, literature, economics, and politics; it is never fashionable to be classical.

CLEAR AND PRESENT DANGER, *n.* A legal doctrine meaning that if a danger is clear it is not necessarily present, and if present it is not necessarily clear. It is the duty of courts to determine which is which, or whether.

CLEAVAGE, *n.* An unseemly public display of a rift between bosom pals.

CLERGYMEN, *n. pl.* Ministers of the Gossipel, according to Scribes and Saints of doubtful veracity.

CLOSE AIR SUPPORT, *n.* In military usage, the air cover given to friendly ground forces who, when the cover is too close, are later identified as such by observing the uniforms of the dead.

CLOSED SEASON, *n.* A period of time during which certain species are protected against the dangers of being hunted or trapped—a protection, unfortunately, that has not been applied to humans.

CLOSED SHOP, *n.* A place that has gone out of business because of redundant labor practices.

CLOSE-MOUTHED, *adj.* Describing a person who communicates more with silence than others do with sound.

CLOSET, *n.* Formerly, a small room used to store clothes, household supplies, and perhaps a family skeleton. Now, a spacious receptacle from which are emerging an astonishing variety of specimens: the gay, the alcoholic, the liberal in the Moral Majority, and the classic case of the closet mole in the CIA.

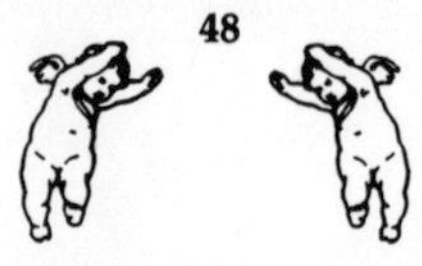

CLOUD NINE, *n.* A piece of real estate in fantasyland that can be reached only on flights of imagination; its inhabitants are dreamers, visionaries, poets, and others considered to be out of this world.

CLOUT, *n.* The most precious possession of politicians and other unscrupulous people who learned hardball on the playing fields of Beat'em.

Some politicians are quiet,
The power behind the throne;
Others live out front,
Among the better known.

Regardless of the style
Or the wickedness of guile,
One thing stands out:
CLOUT!

You've got to have Clout
To chair the right committee,
To get the right bills stopped
And raise a campaign kitty.

You've got to have Clout
To have some foe arrested,
Or have some crime committed
Just as you had requested.

You've got to have Clout
If you want to get the best,
If you want to help your friends
And put your enemies to rest.

It's said that artful compromise
Is what the game is all about,
But when the chips are really down,
Without a qualm, without a doubt,
You've got to show your potent Clout!

GYP GRAFTER

49

Cloud Nine

CLOWN, *n.* A person whose foolish antics and comical appearance make him the star of the circus. In the great circus of politics, most star performers are either born clowns or become that way by imitating their more successful colleagues.

COALITION, *n.* A temporary union of people who differ on all principles except the one of expediency; the only majority party in all democracies.

COAST, *n.,v.* This word means either the land along the sea, or to proceed with a minimum of physical or mental exertion. It is unclear if this accounts for the fact that the United States has a Pacific Coast and a Gulf Coast, but an Atlantic Seaboard.

CO-AUTHOR, *n.* The one who did most of the writing, receives the least praise and most of the criticism.

COCA, *n.* A tropical shrub, the leaves of which impartially provide sips of cola for the parched, and sniffs of cocaine for the bored.

COD LIVER OIL, *n.* A loathsome medicine, rich in vitamins A and D, thus giving rise to the phrase *AD nauseum.*

COEDUCATION, *n.* The lessons that boys and girls learn together in the famous school founded by Adam and Eve.

COERCIONIST, *n.* A person who believes in government by coercion, i.e., anyone who understands what all forms of government have in common.

COFFEE TABLE, *n.* A piece of furniture for the display of books bought to be seen rather than read.

COFFIN CORNER, *n.* (slang) That part of the funereal market monopolized by morticians.

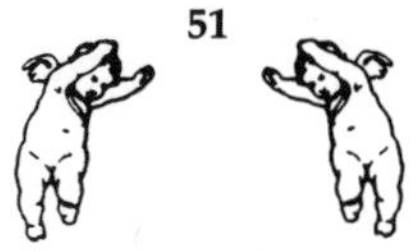

COFFIN NAIL, *n.* (slang) A cigarette, now being hammered senseless by those who have never enjoyed that first puff over the morning coffee.

COINCIDENCE, *n.* The remarkable occurrence of two separate events at the same time, causing people to say that "Life is full of coincidences." Thus it was coincidence that John and Mary became parents at the same time their child was born.

COLA, *n.* A heady drink, especially when bottled as a Cost of Living Adjustment.

COLD COMFORT, *n.* A perfectly made, very dry martini.

Martinis made with gin and wine
Are fine and very nice;
But if you thirst for special thrills
Mix the gin with just dry ice!

Arid Marty

COLLEAGUE, *n.* A friendly associate—after it has been determined that his or her abilities and ambitions do not threaten your own.

COLLECTIVE BARGAINING, *n.* A way of settling labor disputes, whereby the two opposing sides engage in endless talks to impress their respective constituencies. Then a foregone conclusion is reached that permits each bargaining team to claim victory. The principal loser is that larger group known as the public, which gets no bargain at all.

COLLECTIVE NOUN, *n.* One that is singular in form but plural in meaning, except for a word like Congress which is singular, if not downright odd, in both senses.

COLLEGE, *n.* A place where students serve a four-year term without ever being tried or having a single conviction.

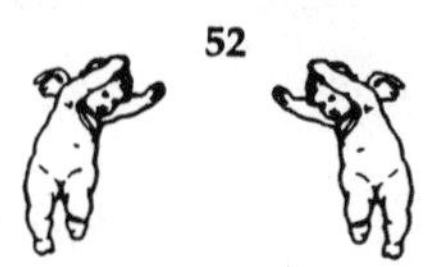

COLLEGE OF CARDINALS, *n.* An organization whose sacred duties are to counsel the living Pope, and to select an old bird to succeed a dead one.

COLORFAST, *adj.* Describing a hunger strike to protest racial discrimination.

COLUMNIST, *n.* A journalist with a buy-line and a license to lie granted by the First Amendment and the Supreme Court of the United States; any heat is avoided by invoking the threat of a "chilling effect" on freedom of the press.

COMBAT FATIGUE, *n.* The mental state of being tired of fighting, a condition so sane and reasonable it is naturally considered to be abnormal by military officials and others whose own sanity is often open to question.

COMMERCIAL TELEVISION, *n.* The kind which, like a prostitute, tries to convince the customer that it's a business doing pleasure, or the reverse.

COMMISSION, *n.* A group of ultra-respectable figureheads selected to study some urgent public problem (which has already been studied *ad nauseum*), with the understanding that its final report will not be taken seriously by anyone after the deadlines have been met, and the headlines have been published.

COMMON CAUSE, *n.* The name of an unusually sanctimonious group that seeks to have an uncommon effect on public affairs, such as taking politics out of politics.

COMMUNISM, *n.* A political, social, and economic philosophy advocating the perfectly reasonable position that property should be shared in common—until one considers his toothbrush and underwear.

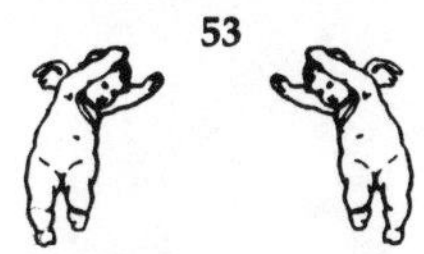

COMPARABLE WORTH, *n.* A recent, controversial proposal, the first serious attempt to determine if apples and oranges can be fruitfully compared. One dilemma was illustrated by the man who, when asked how his wife was, replied, "Compared to what?" and there was no answer.

COMPASSION, *n.* The sentiment of sympathy, kindness, and mercy, which has been injected into modern political rhetoric as one of the loftiest of public themes—which it is easy to do with other people's money.

CONSCIOUSNESS, *n.* A buried quality of mind that all sensitive groups are trying to raise in their own interest. Consciousness raising has become more of an industry than attempts to raise the Titanic.

CONSERVATIVE, *n.* One who believes that all important choices should be made *by* individuals rather than mandated *for* them—except for abortion and prayer in schools.

CONTROVERSIAL, *adj.* Describing any issue about which there is disagreement, which now means everything.

CONVENTIONAL WISDOM, *n.* A periodic form of democratic enlightenment that permits thousands of assembled and confused delegates to nominate two people as candidates for President and Vice President of the United States; more conventional than wise.

CREDIBILITY, *n.* A mysterious substance no political leader, or nation, can afford to lose lest they become even more unbelievable.

CULTURAL RELATIVISM, *n.* The anthropological study of kinship systems and the origin of mother-in-law jokes.

DADAISM, *n.* An exotic movement in modern art and literature, the nature of which is best conveyed by the infantile name it adopted.

DAIRY INDUSTRY, *n.* The one that produces excess milk and cheese products for sale to the United States government in return for federal price supports; in the process the taxpayers get milked more than the cows.

DAIS, *n.* A raised platform at one end of a hall that permits speakers to talk down to their audience, and the audience to look up to them.

DALLAS, *n. pl.* Probably the plural of Dalla which, in contemporary television, signifies endless forms of dalliance, or perhaps a team of cowboys.

DARK AGES, *n. pl.* The ones named thirty, forty, fifty, sixty, etc., as they are successively reached and dreaded.

DARK HORSE, *n.* A person who unexpectedly wins nomination for political office. Fortunately, modern polling tech-

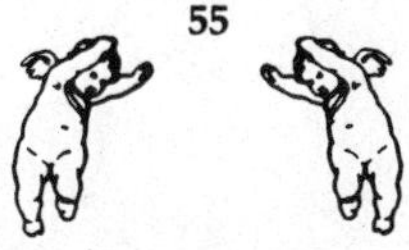

niques leave scant room for this upstart beast, thus clearing the way for real asses.

DASTARDLY, *adj.* Mean, cowardly, sneaky—like any ordinary person.

DAUNTLESS, *adj.* Daring or bold; lacking daunt and a decent fear of the perils of existence.

D-DAY, *n.* A puzzling military expression which, along with H-Hour and M-Minute, is usually credited to a general afflicted with stuttering.

DEAN'S LIST, *n.* The names of faculty members who, in a moment of madness or immodesty, wish to become the new Dean.

> When a Deanship in a certain college became vacant, one faculty member approached the President to put his name up for consideration. "After all," he explained, "I've had twenty years' experience." Somewhat sadly the President replied: "No, not twenty years, one year's experience twenty times." The position remained vacant.

DEATH, *n.* God's way of saying "Hello," while deciding whether to push the Up or Down button.

DEATH BENEFIT, *n.* That ineffable surge of joy experienced upon reading certain obituaries.

> When Franklin D. Roosevelt was President of the United States, he was cordially disliked, if not hated, by many wealthy businessmen—a fact that became the source of one of his favorite stories.
>
> Each morning a Westchester County banker would buy a paper while waiting for his commuter train. Each morning, too, he would lavishly tip the newsboy, take a quick glance at the

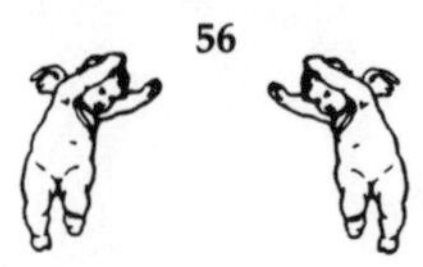

front page, then throw the paper away. Noticing this habit, the newsboy finally asked the banker why he paid so much to only glance at the front page and then discard the whole paper. The banker explained that he was looking for an obituary. "But Mister," the newsboy said, "the obituaries are always in the back pages." "Listen, son," the banker replied, "when the son of a bitch dies that I want to see dead, believe me it'll be headlines on the front page."

DEBATE, *n.* A kind of forum consisting of three main varieties. 1. *Private:* An inner dialogue conducted to convince ourselves that we ought to do what we want to do anyway. 2. *Public:* A discussion of one or more presumably important issues in which both sides are wrong, but no one will admit it. 3. *Presidential:* a side-show staged for the benefit of the suckers.

DE-BRIEFING, *n.* A short military interrogation intended to discover what went wrong.

DEBT, *n.* A financial labyrinth, easy to enter, hard to leave.

Freddie the fool plunged well into debt,
A financial fate he'll never forget;
He suffered much pain
And struggled in vain,
But his income remained gross, not net.

HOCK GREENE

DEBT LIMIT, *n.* The legal ceiling of a government's ability to borrow money; no one yet has hit the ceiling, since it is so easily raised.

DECLARATION, *n.* 1. A ringing, stirring word for a statement. Suppose it had been called The Statement of Independence, or a Statement of War? 2. The statement of lies presented to customs inspectors.

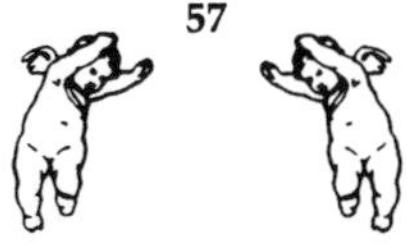

DECLASSIFICATION, *n.* What happens to people who are downwardly mobile, or to documents that are finally downgraded from a previously suspect label of "Top Secret," etc.

DECRIMINALIZATION, *n.* The final recognition that lawmakers had made another mistake.

DEDUCTION, *n.* The painful process of reasoning that leads one to conclude his or her paycheck is smaller.

DEFECTOR, *n.* A person who is given political asylum in one part of the world, as distinguished from a Dissident, who is placed in a medical asylum in another part of the world.

DEFENSE CONTRACTOR, *n.* One who believes that the Pentagon was established solely for executive extravagance, excessive profits, and a pent-up demand for corporate penthouses.

DEGENERATION, *n.* Always the younger one.

DEMAGOGUE, *n.* An ideologue who prefers monologues to dialogues any old day.

DEMOCRACY, *n.* 1. A form of government in which all important officials are elected, and all important decisions are made by unelected officials, such as the Supreme Court, the Chairman of the Federal Reserve Board, and the wife of the President. 2. A popular form of government wherein the people *want* to *admire* their leaders, as distinguished from totalitarianism wherein the people *have* to *adore* their leaders.

DEMOCRATIC PARTY, *n.* In American politics, the party of the people, as opposed to the Republican Party, which is also the party of the people, but the wrong kind.

DEMONSTRATIONS, *n. pl.* The first resort of protesters

more interested in appearing on television than in promoting their cause.

DEMORALIZATION, *n.* The lowering of morale, which moralizing always has the tendency to do.

DEMURE, *adj.* Describing the coy manner affected by sophisticated people for the benefit of the unsuspecting.

DEODORANTS, *n. pl.* Commercial products that can't conceal the malodorousness of the programs they sponsor.

DEPONENT, *n.* In law, a person who gives testimony under oath, usually against an opponent.

DEREGULATION, *n.* A government procedure that permits and encourages the corporate goats to guard the consumers' cabbage patch.

DERMATOLOGY, *n.* A medical specialty that not only gets under your skin, but makes you pay through the nose for the privilege.

DESEGREGATION, *n.* The somewhat illogical attempt to abolish or minimize differences among people by magnifying or exaggerating them.

DESPONDENCY, *n.* The utterly rational feeling of helplessness arising from the shifts, drifts, and rifts of modern life.

DETECTIVE, *n.* One of the heroes of modern fiction, especially if he or she is private, and thus succeeds outside the normal bumbling, fumbling agencies of the law.

DETERRENCE, *n* A widely acclaimed strategy of modern criminology and international relations, the effectiveness of which can only be proved by evidence of its ineffectiveness.

DIAGNOSIS, *n.* The more or less educated guess made by a physician as to which school of illnesses your symptoms are attending.

I weighed my fate, and lost the weight,
Just as the doctors said;
And when I reached that pearly gate
My weight was down, but I was dead.

I still paid heed and quit the weed,
Just as the doctors said;
My lungs were clear when refereed
But, still, I was quite dead.

Don't think too much, or drink too much,
The serious doctors said;
But when I felt that final touch
The doctors, too, were all quite dead.

MORT ALWORTHY

Show me a person who doesn't smoke or drink, who watches his weight, exercises regularly, avoids stress, and has an annual medical checkup—and soon I will show you a very healthy corpse.

HARDY B. FITT

DIALOGUE, *n.* An interchange of opinions and ideas, consisting of two or more monologues that meander right past each other without even nodding.

DICTIONARY, *n.* The only non-fiction publication that requires neither an index or a table of contents.

DIET, *n.* A miserable thing that one is either going on or off of, sometimes simultaneously.

DIGNITARIES, *n. pl.* All those nameless, faceless people who appear at public rituals with nothing to do, and who would benefit everyone by the absence of their presence.

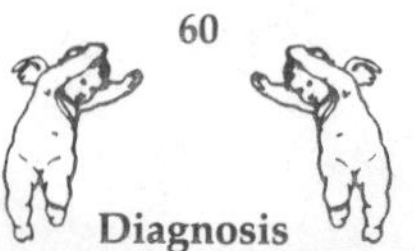

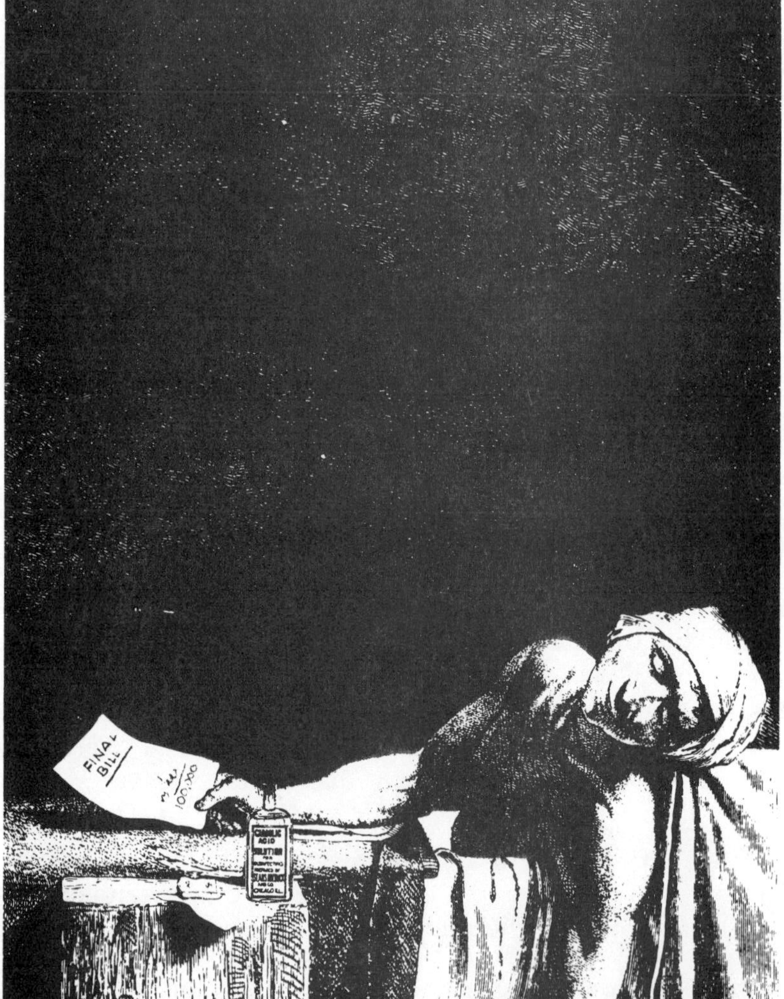

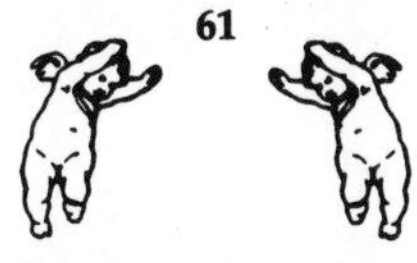

DIGNITY, *n.* That quality of pride, worth, or honor frequently and erroneously attributed to a person (usually a stuffed shirt), or an office (such as a court or the presidency), both of which are notoriously deficient in this regard. This moral fraud has recently been extended and compounded by the claim that all peoples possess "human dignity," as revealed, no doubt, by the greed, lust, brutality, tyranny, and depravity displayed by man in all times and places, and under all social and political systems.

DILEMMA, *n.* Any situation requiring a choice between disagreeable alternatives, such as voting, turning on the television set, or selecting a dentist.

DIPLOMACY, *n.* The fine art of being able to lie with a straight face and a crooked mind.

DIPLOMATIC IMMUNITY, *n.* A code recognized by all nations, whereby the personnel of all foreign embassies are immune from arrest or punishment for breaking laws of the host nation. This is justified on the basis of national interest: if we protect their personnel, they will protect ours. In reality, another reason is paramount. Embassy officials are members of government, and the people must never be allowed to forget that government officials, even of foreign nations, are always above the law.

DIRTY LINEN, *n.* The kind that should never be washed in public. The fact that clean linen should never be soiled there either is usually overlooked.

DISASTER, *n.* The daily state of the world as perceived and portrayed by the news media in their persistent efforts to keep us uninformed and unenlightened.

DISBARMENT, *n.* The punishment occasionally inflicted upon lawyers when caught in the practice of their usual chicanery.

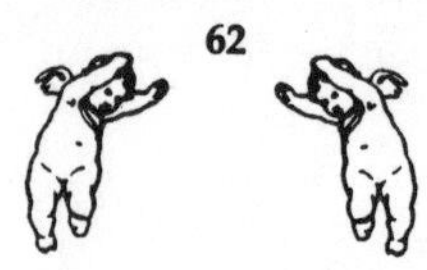

DISCERNING, *adj.* Astute, showing good judgment; what is said of people whose thought bears a remarkable resemblance to our own.

DISCIPLINE, *n.* The training that promotes the development of good character and which is, therefore, conspicuously absent in families and public schools.

DISCRETION, *n.* The freedom to make decisions, so long as they are cautious, prudent, and cost-effective.

DIVISIVENESS, *n.* A phenomenon rightly feared by the leaders of all groups because it reveals the bad feelings existing among members who do not like each other, i.e., the normal state of affairs.

DIVORCE, *n.* The final, legal signal that something is troubling a marriage, and pleasing the lawyers.

DNA, *n.* Pronounced D,N,A; the name given to Deoxyribonucleic acid, when it was discovered that the latter was too long to fit into the chromosome of which it was supposed to be a part.

DOCTRINAIRE, *adj.* The dogmatic adherence to a doctrine of some kind. If this did not happen, the doctrine would lose its air and there would be no one left to indoctrinate.

DOGHOUSE, *n.* A gravely over-crowded shelter, the place where people in disfavor are put. People in favor are permitted to roam aimlessly until they say or do the wrong thing.

DOUBLE AGENT, *n.* A spy who spies on spies and gets paid twice, once by each side; the prototype of the double cross, and the stuff of novels and legends.

> International espionage is a fact of life in the modern (and not so modern) world. Each na-

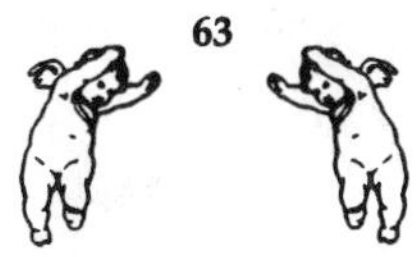

tion has its agents spying busily on friend and foe alike. Some remain true to the country that hires them; others become double, triple or, for all I know, quadruple agents. Regardless of the multiples, it is generally agreed that spying is a most dangerous profession, especially if one is caught, and that the rewards to its practitioners include prestige as well as money. Yes, there is a status system within the fraternity of spies.

This was well illustrated when Nathan and Blinkman, each ostensibly in the hire of hostile governments, were both captured by still a third government. Officials made it clear that they would both be killed if they did not inform on all other agents known to them—their networks and controls. Now, quite contrary to popular myth, spies seldom prefer death to disclosure, and so it happened that Nathan and Blinkman told all they knew. Soon they were released and returned to the underground world which was their life.

Rather quickly it became known throughout the community of spies that Blinkman had in fact been a triple agent, and thus had disclosed the existence of three networks to Nathan's pitiful one. Blinkman's status soared, Nathan's declined.

Such were the real circumstances surrounding Nathan's historic remark, "I regret that I had but one country to give for my life."

POLTER M. GEIST

DOUBLE STANDARD, *n.* The widely criticized moral code that is stricter for women than for men, whereas it should be the reverse.

DOUBLE TALK, *n.* What is heard from a two-faced person.

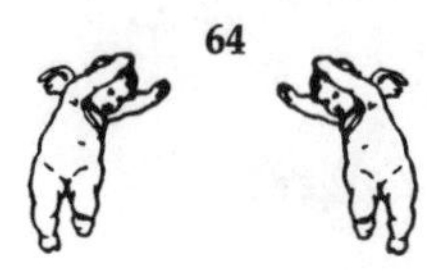

DREAMS, *n. pl.* 1. A form of fantasy. Occurring at night they interfere with sleep, at day with promotion. 2. The phenomena that made Freud famous, and vice versa.

DUE PROCESS, *n.* A priceless legal doctrine designed to assure that nothing undue will happen to the guilty.

DUPLICATING MACHINE, *n.* A prodigious modern invention that has multiplied the amount of paper work in circulation by providing many more copies than are necessary; a miracle, or monster, of reproduction.

DURABLE, *adj.* Lasting or enduring, except in the case of what economists call "durable goods" (appliances, furniture, etc.) which are ticketed for early obsolescence.

DYE, *n.* A colorful ingredient of the modern coiffure.

> Not long ago in a certain community, the dyemakers union hosted a luncheon for the leading citizens and politicians. It would not have rated even a footnote in local history, were it not for the master of ceremonies who opened the occasion by saying: "We who are about to salad you, dye—hair today and lawn tomorrow." The lynching is still talked about.
>
> PUNCH AGONER

EAR, *n.* A rather unshapely sense organ, used more for hearing than listening, especially when *you* are talking.

> A famous politician spent many tedious hours in reception lines. As each person moved by, he would shake the extended hand, make some idle remark, and be rewarded with an equally inane reply. Very early in his career he began to realize that no one was really listening or paying attention to what was being said.
>
> Thereafter, to relieve the boredom from time to time, he would say, while shaking someone's hand, "You know, I robbed a store last night." "Fine, fine, I'm glad to hear it," the person would respond. The politician hugely enjoyed this private joke. He was Franklin D. Roosevelt.

EARNEST MONEY, *n.* The up-front payment one gives an attorney to buy his serious attention to the problem at hand; more a hope than a promise.

EARSHOT, *n.* The distance within which a sound can be heard, too short for things you don't want to hear, like crit-

icism, and too long for things you do want to hear, like praise.

EAVESDROP, *v.* An impolite but effective way of discovering other people's secrets without revealing your own.

ECCENTRICITY, *n.* An irritating trait of other people; our own eccentricities are harmless and charming.

ECONOMICS, *n.* The "dismal science," more dismal than science, and more exasperating in language and logic than exact in conclusions. As currently practiced, it resembles the definition Bertrand Russell once gave of mathematics: a subject "in which we never know what we are talking about, nor whether what we are saying is true." Yet all modern governments think it necessary to have economic advisers.

ECONOMIC SUMMIT, *n.* A meeting attended by the heads of major industrial nations, who know nothing about economics. They are aided by advisers who also know nothing about economics—which is just as well, since few decisions are actually made and the amount of damage done is thereby contained.

ECUMENICAL, *adj.* Describing the effort made to further religious unity, especially among Christians. Historically, the two favorite methods have been conversion and coercion, with the latter predominating in the form of massacre and torture. The thought was that if enough heretics were killed off, the survivors would embrace unity gladly.

EDEN, *n.* A biblical garden where Eve learned all about apples and Adam learned all about Eve.

EDITORIALS, *n. pl.* The opinions of editors and publishers that are reflected in all news columns and the columns of advertising revenues.

EDUCATION, *n.* In the United States, a quaint way of

67

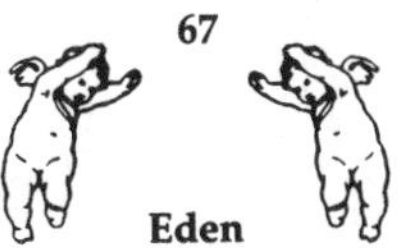

Eden

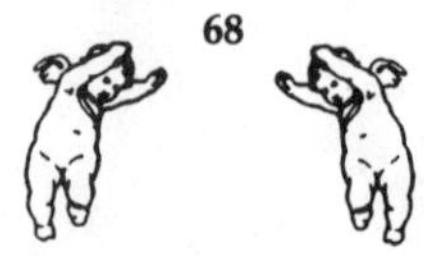

identifying knowledge by counting the number of credits and credentials collected.

EDUCATIONAL THEORY, *n.* 1. A deplorable subject, taught badly at all schools and colleges of education because there is nothing to teach. 2. A curious mode of thought and inquiry, the principal conclusion of which has been that one need not be a criminal to teach criminology, nor be an engine to become an engineer.

EFFEMINATE, *adj.* Showing qualities attributed to women, such as weakness and fragility, best demonstrated by the capacity to bear children and outlive men.

To call a man effeminate
Commits a serious wrong,
Unless he proves by every bit
That he is tough and strong.
Be not misled by idle talk
About the weaker sex:
When they are just beginning,
Already men are wrecks.

MAUDE GENDRE

EGALITARIAN, *adj.* Advocating full political and social equality for all people, which is safe to do since its impossibility precludes having to live with its consequences. How could we have envy or excellence, scorn or scandals, if everyone were equal?

EGOCENTRIC, *adj.* Viewing all things in relation to oneself—selfish perhaps, but with a certain survival value.

EIGHTEEN, *n., adj.* Eight more than ten, and two less than twenty—an awkward number as is demonstrated by adolescence.

ELECTION, *n.* In democracies, a way of changing the cast of a political comedy, without affecting the performance.

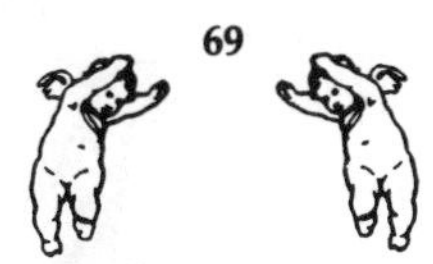

ELECTRICITY, *n.* Always a matter of current affairs, knowledge of which begins and ends with turning a switch or pushing a button.

ELITISM, *n.* The view that a few superior people are best equipped to handle public affairs. This is heresy to democratic peoples who then proceed to create the Imperial Presidency, the Honorable Court, Lords of the Press, and other manifestations of the common man.

ELOPE, *v.* To run away secretly to get married, something like breaking into jail.

EMBASSY, *n.* An ambassador and the staff, whose main task is to await further instructions from the home country in order to find out what in the hell they are doing in such a strange place.

EMBROIL, *v.* To involve in trouble, as typically occurs with a piece of meat at a backyard barbecue.

EMPEROR, *n.* The supreme ruler of an empire, after the empress.

ENCOUNTER GROUP, *n.* A regrettable recent invention in which one is encouraged to receive psychological therapy by encountering, in the strangest ways, even stranger people than might ordinarily be encountered.

ENEMY, *n.* A person or nation that has come to its senses just in time.

ENFORCE, *v.* To compel observance of the law. Nothing pleases voters more than to hear a candidate promise to enforce the law—as long as it's against someone else.

ENGAGE, *v.* To enter into conflict, which is why couples are said to become engaged to marry.

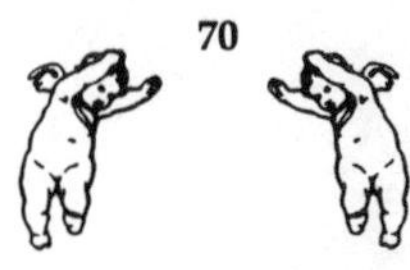

ENGLISH, *n.* A dead language, murdered by journalists, bureaucrats, social scientists, and English teachers.

ENJOIN, *v.* To prohibit by legal injunction—which courts enjoy doing because it enriches some, enrages others, and enhances their own sense of power.

ENLIGHTENMENT, *n.* The unsuccessful effort to free people from ignorance, prejudice, superstition, and other enduring elements of human nature.

ENOUGH, *adj.* As much as may be sufficient unto the needs of the day—which it never is.

There's never enough of anything
To really go around;
It's because of scarce resources
That utopias run aground.
To be satisfied with less
Goes strong against our grain,
For thoughts of ever more
Are dancing through the brain.
And that's the final word
About the human lot:
If more can be envisioned
Whatever is enough is not!

ORRIS SADLY

ENTERTAIN, *v.* Either to amuse, or to consider. Public education has the policy of entertaining students rather than instructing them, and will not entertain the thought that learning might be difficult.

ENTITLEMENTS, *n. pl.* Originally, these were certain privileges, such as social security or military pensions, which have now become legally mandated regardless of need or merit. To paraphrase Anatole France, "The law in its majestic impartiality permits the rich as well as the poor to receive social security benefits or government pensions."

ENTRAPMENT, *n.* An attractive method used by law enforcement officials to entice law-abiding citizens to break the law.

ENTREPRENEUR, *n.* A person who is willing to take risks for the sake of profits, like thieves or bank robbers.

ENVIRONMENTALIST, *n.* A person who loudly and endlessly proclaims that he or she is more concerned about the environment than anyone else who is living in it.

ENVY, *n.* The perfectly normal desire for anything another may have, particularly his envy.

EPIC, *n.* A long dramatic poem about the great deeds of heroes and heroines—which is about the only place they can still be found.

EPICURE, *n.* A person who has the good taste to prefer a dry martini to a wet one, and ham to hamburger.

EPILOGUE, *n.* A brief section added to a book or a play wherein the author explains what all the preceding pages were about.

EPISTLES, *n. pl.* What New Testament authors wrote instead of letters.

EQUAL, *adj.* Ideally, what all men created are, but creation is neither birth nor life, and in these crucibles all are equally unequal in some capacity.

EQUIVOCATE, *v.* To use ambiguous or equivocal words and phrases to mislead or confuse; a variant of advocate.

ERA, *n.* Formerly, an historical period distinguished for significant events. Now, when separated into E,R,A, it is either the earned run average of a baseball pitcher, or an

Equal Rights Amendment, whichever is more applicable to the season.

ERASER, *n.* A handy means for correcting errors in writing or 'rithmetic, but not available for errors in life.

EROTICA, *n.* The expensive, legal, respectable class of pornography, as distinguished from the cheap, vulgar, illegal, hard-core kind.

Some books were dirty
Some books were clean;
Others were listed
As in between.
The dirty books
Began to sell,
The sales of others
Slowed and fell.
Authors learned
Just what it took
To give their books
A dirty look.
Censors rose
In mighty wrath,
Declaring books
Required a bath.
Laws were passed
With righteous wails
To send the rogues
To dirty jails.
The courts stepped in
To take a look
At what was called
A dirty book.
The judges read
And most took heed:
Does it matter
What we read?
Right they were
In what they saw,

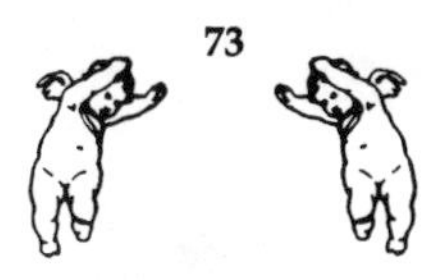

Not all dirt's
Against the law.
So that's the tale
Of censorship
And its fateful
Legal trip.
Censors fail
When freedom's there,
And freedom's there
To clear the air.

I. F. BEHOLDER

ERR, *v.* To be wrong or mistaken. To err is human; not to err is inhuman.

ESTABLISHMENT, *n.* In modern usage, an inner circle of the elite, thought to hold decisive power in all matters of importance. Its existence has not yet been proven, which means it must be doing something right as well as wrong.

ESTIMATES, *n. pl.* The disputable "facts" of modern life, calculated by unknown people, in unknown ways, but cited frequently enough to be accepted as truth, whereupon they become the basis for all manner of laws and public policies.

> "Let who will be law and policy makers, so long as I can make the estimates." Anon.

ETC. (Latin, short for *et cetera,* meaning "and so forth.") The name to be given to sequels of the movie, *E.T.*

ETERNITY, *n.* That endless amount of time one spends awaiting the arrival of the doctor or the tax refund.

ETHICS, *n. pl.* A region of morality existing somewhere between law and custom, with the force of neither. Codes of professional ethics are belated efforts to admonish practitioners about their sins, and to advise them as to avoidance and expiation.

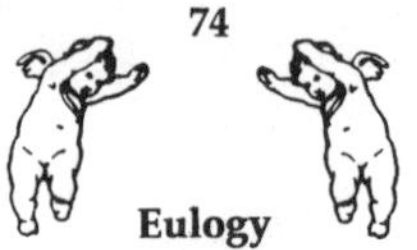

Eulogy

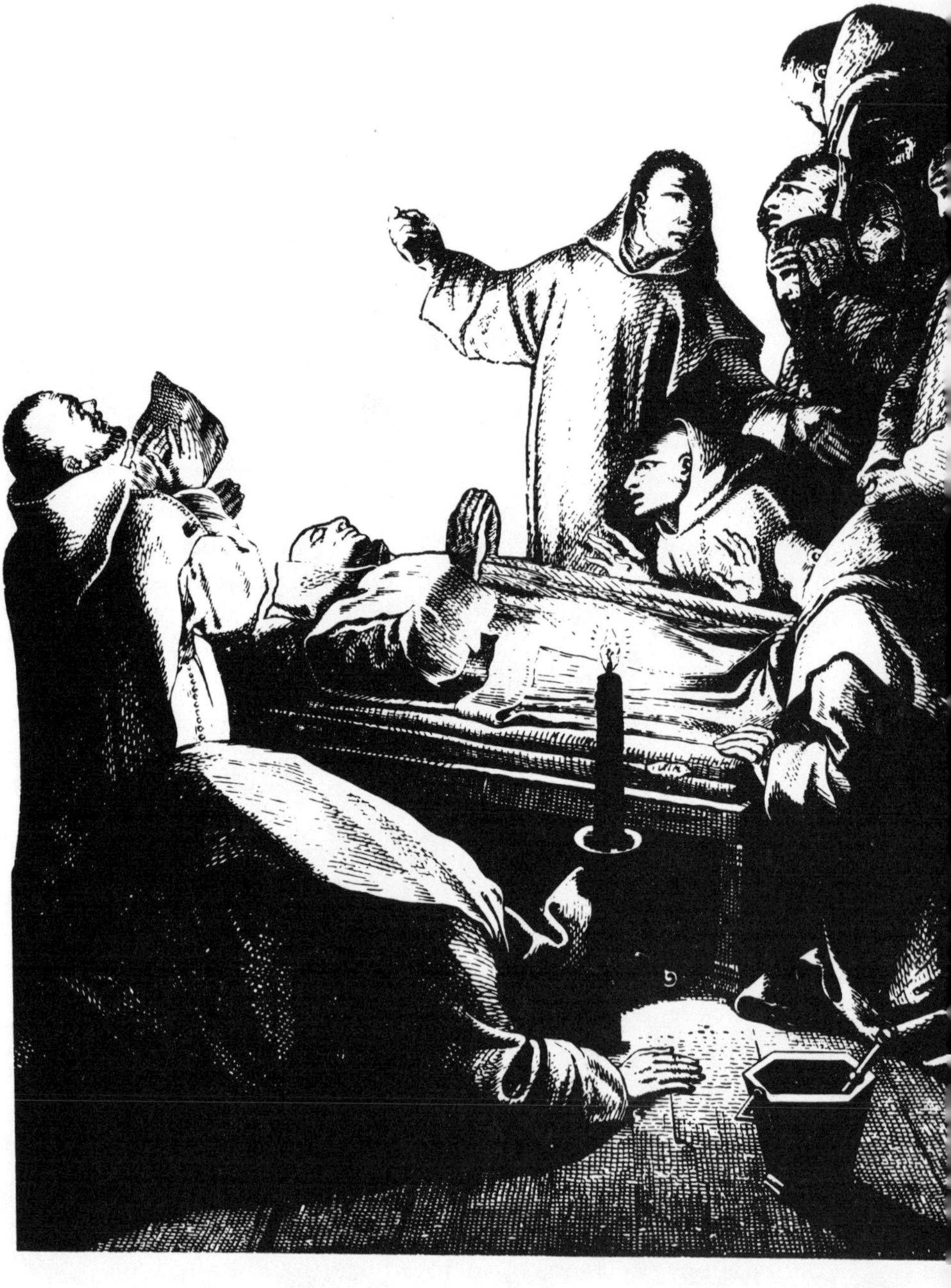

EULOGY, *n.* A funeral oration that ignores the sins, praises the sinner, and alerts the saints to a new arrival.

EUPHEMISM, *n.* Language that has been laundered to come out clean.

EUTHANASIA, *n.* A euphemism for justifiable homicide, i.e., merciful death. Naturally, it is condemned by our uncivilization which prefers suffering and longevity to humane pity.

EXCELLENCE, *n.* The invidious condition of superiority achieved by some people in order to make merely good people look bad.

EXEMPTION, *n.* The condition of being free from the rules and obligations that apply to others, e.g., legal tax exemption, which is more highly prized than religious redemption.

EXPERIENCE, *n.* What is gained in the process of moving from the familiar to the strange, until the latter becomes the former.

EXPERT, *n.* A modern seer, often self-styled, whose pronouncements are received as if emanating from an oracle. A "recognized expert" is one whose pronouncements are closest to conventional wisdom.

EXPLANATION, *n.* A polite way of forestalling any more vexatious questions. This was best illustrated by the immortal line of Ring Lardner: when a child asked his father an irritating question, the response was: " 'Shut up,' he explained."

EXPLETIVE, *n.* A coarse oath which, as the White House tapes taught us, sounds better when deleted.

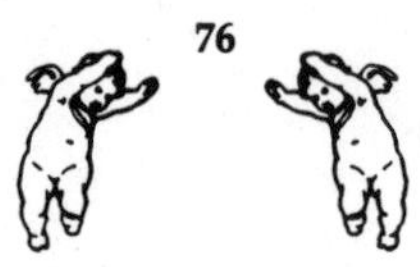

EXTORTION, *n.* Obtaining money from someone by force or threats. This is a crime, except in the case of the Internal Revenue Service where it is known as "voluntary compliance."

EXTROVERT, *n.* A personality type, imagined by psychologists, thought to be more interested in others than in himself.

EYEWITNESS, *n.* A person whose testimony is uncontradicted in direct proportion to his being the sole one.

FACE-LIFT, *n.* The modern, surgical way of saving face by putting on a better one.

FACE-OFF, *n.* The process, involving sticks and a puck, which opposing players use to start a hockey match—and which some players almost end with.

FACE VALUE, *n.* The source of income found in the cosmetics industry.

FACT, *n.* A fiction taken to be a matter of truth by one or another faction.

FACULTY, *n.* Formerly, an assembly of independent scholars and teachers; now, the same people who have become more interested in earning than learning, and who discovered that in their union there is strength.

"I've lost my faculties,"
The college president moaned.
"Not at all," the dean replied,
"The union bargained on their side
And now they all are cloned."

WILEY JAKLE

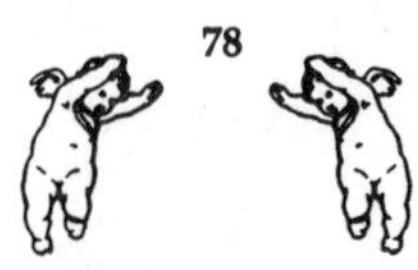

FAIL-SAFE, *adj.* A shorthand way of saying that if the control systems fail, you're not safe.

FAIRNESS, *n.* That impartiality and equity of treatment that everyone approves of, so long as their own interests are not threatened.

FAIRY TALE, *n.* The unbelievable story contained in an official report.

FALLIBLE, *adj.* Liable to be mistaken, as distinguished from gullible, which means liable to be taken.

FALSEHOOD, *n.* A lie. It comes in three varieties: downright, bare-faced, and statistical.

FAME, *n.* That which results from positive publicity as opposed to shame, which results from negative publicity. Notoriety results from any kind of publicity at all. Like triplets, they are often mistaken for each other because the similarities outweigh their differences.

FAMILY ROOM, *n.* What the bathroom becomes as soon as one wishes to use it.

FANATICISM, *n.* The stubborn difference between a true believer and a true belief.

FANFARE, *n.* The price people pay to keep athletes and entertainers in the luxury to which they are accustomed.

FAST FOOD, *n.* The kind that nutritionists and slow eaters complain about, the former because it endangers health, the latter because of indigestion.

FAST LANE, *n.* A modern metaphor for the highway of life—either a swift passage on the road to success, or just another primrose path, depending on the driver and his or her direction.

FAT CAT, *n.* (slang) A wealthy political contributor waiting to be lionized.

FATES, *n. pl.* In Greek and Roman mythology, the three goddesses thought to control human life and destiny, now most familiarly known as religion, science, and government.

FATHER-IN-LAW, *n.* The only relative acquired by marriage who does not automatically become a joke.

FATHERLAND, *n.* What the Germans call their nation, whereas in the Soviet Union it is Mother Russia. Both have given parenthood a bad name among nations.

FATUOUS, *adj.* Preposterously foolish and stupid, which is why it is said politicians live off the fatuous of the land.

FAULT, *n.* A blame we should always be generous to, especially our own.

FBI, *n.* The Federal Bureau of Investigation. For many decades it was known unofficially as Hoover's private vacuum cleaner for picking up dirt on public officials and other types of criminals.

FEDERALIZE, *v.* To put under federal authority; not to be confused with fertilize, which means to make fruitful.

FEEDBACK, *n.* In technical language, feedback occurs when part of the output becomes another input. In nontechnical life, it is what fed-up people deliver to those doing the feeding out.

FEELING, *n.* That which people speak with when they are being particularly insincere.

FELLOWSHIP, *n.* In academic life, the recognition that scholarship plus grantsmanship equals sponsorship.

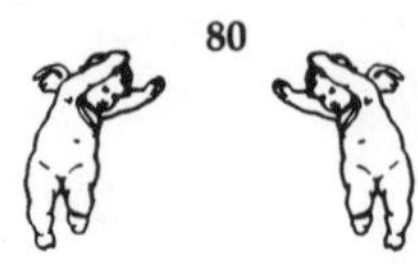

FELLOW TRAVELER, *n.* A person who refrains from entering the vehicle, but goes in the same direction in the left lane on the political highway.

FEMINIST, *n.* 1. An emancipated woman who will skirt every issue. 2. An emancipated woman who won't.

FEUD, *n.* An enduring quarrel. In medieval Europe, this gave rise to feudalism, based on quarrels between serfs and masters. According to Marx, this was replaced by capitalism, which is based on quarrels between capitalists and laborers, and between Marxists and non-Marxists.

FIFTH AMENDMENT, *n.* A serious change in a revered American institution, occurring when a bottle of scotch became .75 liters.

A fifth of scotch was common tongue,
Its virtues touted, often sung;
We had our fifth on the Fourth of July,
Along with the fireworks lighting the sky;
But now that liters are the name of the game,
The Fourth of July is just not the same,
Nor is the scotch that we all used to buy.

QUINTUS QUIRK

FIGUREHEAD, *n.* A titular leader who has no power; a deadhead of authority.

FILMSTRIP, *n.* A soft-porn movie, which might earn a PG rating if tastefully done.

FINANCE, *n.* Large money resources, usually found in two places: the highworld and the underworld.

FIRST GENTLEMAN, *n.* What the husband of a woman President of the United States will be known as. ("The President and the gracious First Gentleman spent the weekend at Camp David.")

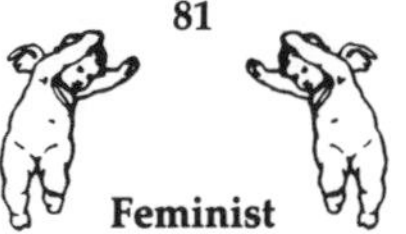

81

Feminist

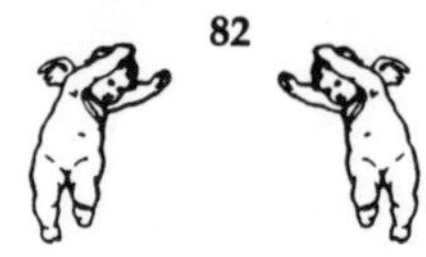

FIRST-RATE, *adj.* Describing anything that is slightly ahead of second-rate, with the latter fast closing in as standards continue to decline.

FIRST STRIKE, *n.* Either the beginning of the ballgame or the end, depending upon what is being hurled.

FISSION, *n.* A splitting apart. When joined with the word nuclear, it means the whole world has gone fission, with nothing to catch.

FLAG, *n.* A piece of colored cloth which people rally around as a signal that something troublesome, like a war or an election, is taking place.

FLIGHT, *n.* A useful alternative to fight, especially if you can outrun the enemy. ("He who fights and runs away, lives to fight some other day.")

FLOOR WALKER, *n.* Either a new parent, or one with an adolescent in the family.

FLOUT, *v.* To mock or scorn, as distinguished from flaunt, which means to show off proudly. The two are often confused, but this is easily remedied. One need only remember that a person can flaunt a flout, but not the reverse, and a person can flout convention and flaunt non-conformity at the same time.

FLU, *n.* A mysterious illness that is spread less by the viruses going around than by word that it's going around.

FLUNKY, *n.* A person who failed in school, but learned to survive anyway.

FLUSH, *v., n.* To blush or glow, or a winning hand at poker, provided one does not do the first while holding the second.

FLYING SAUCER, *n.* An unidentified flying object, said to be seen only by people in their cups or on the sauce. This is disputed by those who caught the flight.

FODDER, *n.* The helpless soldiers that cannon eat regularly, and with relish, in the gruesome meals of war.

FOIBLE, *n.* A small weakness in character that becomes a major vice when found irritating. Among the irritating foibles of Aesop was his habit of finding moral lessons in the amoral behavior of animals.

FOLLY, *n.* Foolishness—a commodity which is always abundant, regardless of whatever else is scarce.

FOOTNOTES, *n. pl.* The spiciest parts of history, and therefore the most difficult to find.

FORESIGHT, *n.* A prudent regard for the future which, if distant enough, is called farsightedness.

FOREST, *n.* Something that can't be seen because of those infernal trees that obscure philosophical vision. 2. Nature's way of assuring that we have something to read, regardless of merit.

FORGIVE, *v.* What politicians proudly do to their enemies, but without either forgetting or forewarning them.

We should be kind and generous
To enemies we may have;
It's not all that onerous
To apply some soothing salve.

But just when they feel easy,
And think we've lost our clout,
That's the time to strike
And knock the bastards out.

HARDY SLUGG

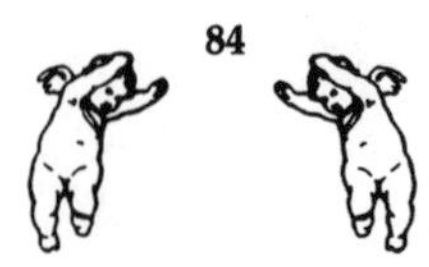

FOUNDATION, *n.* A philanthropic institution dedicated to doing good tax-exempt deeds, like sponsoring more research on a problem that's already well understood. It is the business of foundation executives to decide not only who should do the research, but also who can write the dullest report.

FOUR-LETTER WORDS, *n. pl.* The famous ones so long forbidden in books, on the screen, or in polite company. Now they are paraded everywhere, except for love, unless used as a synonym for lust.

FOURTH WORLD, *n.* The desolate one following the Third World War.

FRAG, *v.* (military slang) To intentionally wound or kill a superior officer, an activity in which it is easy to enlist much help.

FRANKFURTER, *n.* The great American hot dog, which is always served cold. A Supreme Court Justice with this name was called, with great relish by his opponents, the Hot Dog from Harvard, where he had been a law professor.

FREEDOM, *n.* A glorious condition of existence, best known and appreciated by prolonged exposure to its absence; otherwise it is so invisible as to be unnoticed.

FREE LUNCH, *n.* What people constantly tell us there is no such thing as, while someone else picks up their check.

FREE WILL, *n.* A tax-free bequest, as opposed to determinism which specifies the precise amount due.

FREEZE, *n.* Icy when natural, nicer when nuclear.

FREIGHT, *n.* The transporting of goods; if by sea, it's called cargo, if by land, it's a shipment. Just why this is so is not manifest.

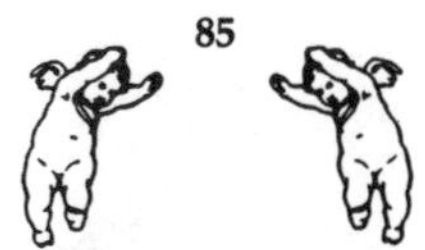

FRIEND, *n.* A splendid person who nearly always understands your faults, and overstates your virtues.

FRINGE BENEFITS, *n. pl.* The ones that are fast becoming more valuable and important than the one in the center, which is only salary.

FRONTIERS, *n. pl.* The outer rims of learning or science, beyond which is the unknown, i.e., practically everything. They are conquered by inspired people who use cutting edges to achieve breakthroughs.

FRUGAL, *adj.* Prudent and thrifty, which is a good thing to be: no one knows what crazy things Congress or the IRS will do next with your income.

> A schoolteacher was in the habit of requiring her students to write a brief essay illustrating a key word. One day the word was "frugal," the meaning of which was completely unknown to one in the class. He sought help, but his friend only had time to whisper, "Save, save."
>
> The teacher noticed this exchange, so the lad who had asked for help was called on first to read his essay.
>
> "Once upon a time," the boy read, "a beautiful princess lived in a castle near a forest. While walking in the forest one day, a horrible dragon caught her. 'Frugal me, frugal me,' she cried. A handsome prince saved her, and they lived frugally ever after."
>
> ELSIE WORTHMORE

FUTURE, *n.* A point in time beyond our seers, but not our fears.

GAG LAW, *n.* What the press calls any rule or court order that sticks in its insatiable throat.

GALAHAD, *n.* In the Arthurian legend, the chaste knight who found the Holy Grail after much chasing about. Others may also have found it had they tried as hard as Galahad.

GAMBIT, *n.* Any action intended to gain an advantage, meaning that most human action consists of opening or closing gambits.

GAME, *n.* An entertaining way of making enemies out of friends.

GAME THEORY, *n.* A sporting mathematical method that, among other things, tells us (hypothetically, of course) how to minimize maximum losses in a nuclear war.

GAMUT, *n.* The entire range of something. Dorothy Parker once remarked of a certain well-known actress, "She ran the gamut of emotions from A to B." In a different vein, there is growing agreement among scholars that human history has run the gamut from idiocy to imbecility.

GAP, *n.* A modern buzz word pointing toward allegedly serious discontinuities or intervals between things: the missile gap, knowledge gap, education gap, generation gap, gender gap, etc.

GARBAGE, *n.* The waste that civilization finds easy to produce, difficult to collect, and all but impossible to dispose of.

GAY, *n.* A person who, upon coming out of a dark closet, found that his or her life-style was quite fashionable after all.

GENDER, *n.* A recently revitalized word meaning that people should search for what engendered their own sexuality.

GENERAL PRACTITIONER, *n.* 1. A physician who will practice medicine on anyone without a specialized disease. 2. A high ranking military doctor.

GENESIS, *n.* The first book of the Bible, since it all had to start somewhere.

GENIUS, *n.* A superior talent a person is known to have, in retrospect.

GERMICIDE, *n.* A substance invented in two world wars for the purpose of killing Germans before they killed us.

GET AWAY, *v.* To escape from, which is all right, but not nearly as good as to get away with.

GETTING AHEAD, *v.* A preoccupation of middle class Americans and some South American tribes. When the Americans succeed, the head swells; with the tribes, it shrinks.

88

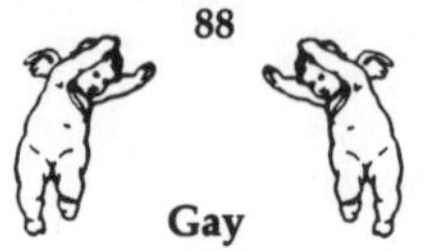

Gay

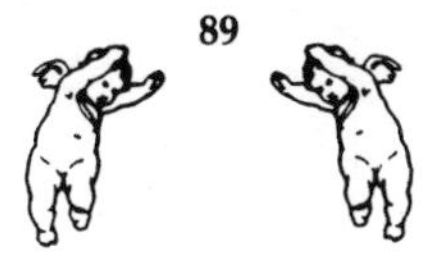

GETTYSBURG, *n.* A place that has the distinction of being both the address of a famous battle scene, and the scene of an even more famous address.

GHOST WRITER, *n.* A friendly person who lets someone else take credit for his work, while he takes the cash.

GIANT, *adj.* The regular size of sales, rallies, and cereal boxes.

GIFTED, *adj.* A word used by critics to describe an author or performer they find too promising to disparage, and too disappointing to promote.

GILT-EDGED, *adj.* Of highest quality, when not also guilt-edged.

GIMMICK, *n.* A tricky, deceptive device; that without which no candidate can be elected, no commercial made, nor any product sold.

GIRL SCOUT, *n.* A member of a character-building organization devoted to selling cookies and walking in civic parades.

GLADIATOR, *n.* What a laconic alligator is reported to have said when questioned about the disappearance of a female swimmer.

GLAMOR, *n.* The unidentifiable quality that gives to those who have it all the identity they need.

GLEE CLUB, *n.* A singing group that provides a great deal of glee to those out of earshot.

GLORY, *n.* The fame and honor that is lost by failure, sought by ambition, found by chance, and rewarded with success.

GOBBLEDYGOOK, *n.* A sub-species of gibberish, in that it is usually confined to bureaucrats and politicians, whereas gibberish, a close cousin of jargon, is widely dispersed throughout modern culture.

GOD, *n.* 1. A celestial committee—no single Deity alone could have screwed up the world so thoroughly. 2. A Deity who not only played dice with the universe (contrary to Einstein) but loaded them on the side of sin.

GODFATHER, *n.* A once honorific title that has now fallen into profitable disrepute.

GODIVA, *n.* A brave lady who, to demonstrate the result of heavy taxes, rode naked through the streets of Coventry, only to find the IRS waiting for her with a camera.

GOLD, *n.* The way touring professional golfers spell golf.

GOOD FRIDAY, *n.* The quaint name for a day commemorating a rather gruesome crucifixion. Christian theologians are still in disagreement about criteria for a Bad Friday.

GOOD SAMARITAN, *n.* A person who generously and unselfishly helps others—a practice so suspect and dangerous that many states have laws to protect doctors and others who attempt it.

GOOD WILL, *n.* One that leaves you something, as opposed to Bad Will, in which lawyers and/or the state get it all.

GOP, *n.* The letters standing for the Republican, or Grand Old Party. Once thought to be the Gone Old Party, it has recently been referred to as GYP, or the Growing Young Party.

GOSPEL, *n.* A type of Christian truth that requires authority for legitimacy and belief for proof.

GOVERNMENT, *n.* The ubiquitous political arm of society. Right or left, it always has muscle, a crooked elbow, and a clenched fist.

GRAFFITI, *n.* Memorable art too good to be published, so it brightens the otherwise dull walls of toilets, subway stations, and vacant buildings.

GRAFT, *n.* The corrupting lubricant of society, i.e., what really makes big government, big business, and big labor work together, as badly as they do.

GRAMMAR SCHOOL, *n.* An obsolete educational institution; so is good grammar.

GRAND JURY, *n.* An officious legal body whose indictments grandly set in motion the wayward wheels of justice.

GRAPHOLOGY, *n.* The pseudo-science of handwriting and its relation to character; phrenology moved from the head to the hand.

GRASS ROOTS, *n. pl.*, (colloquial) The basis of a certain kind of euphoria common to politics and marijuana users.

GRATITUDE, *n.* Thankful appreciation expressed for the pleasure of appearing grateful.

GRAY MATTER, *n.* A colloquial term for intelligence, so used because of the vague, indeterminate area it designates.

> An English professor, with a droll sense of humor, was fond of giving unannounced spot quizzes. On one such occasion, a student who had done no studying at all received the quiz book, carefully wrote on the cover the name of the course, the date, the name of the professor and his own name. On the inside first page, with

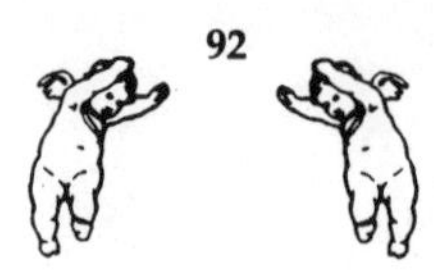

equal care, he wrote "1," leaving everything else blank. When the quiz books were returned, a large F, in red, was on the cover. On the first page inside, was carefully written: "Too vague."

GREENHORN, *n.* An inexperienced person, easily duped by people who blow their own.

GROOM, *v.* To train a person for proper performance, which is why a newly married man is known as a bridegroom—the bride will do the grooming.

GROSS NATIONAL PRODUCT, or GNP, *n.* The total value of a nation's annual output of goods and services which, since it is always unknown and unknowable, is a favored concept of economists; another one of those estimates that can be grossly under- or over-stated, and who's to know?

GRUDGE, *n.* The ill will you hold against people whom you have wronged, and which they begrudgingly acknowledge.

GUILT, *n.* The sense of sin as seen through your own eyes, as distinguished from shame, which is the same thing viewed through the eyes of others.

HABITS, *n. pl.* The daily routines employed to prevent overworking a brain that is already tired enough.

HABITAT, *n.* The comfortable dwelling of a creature of habit.

HACKER, *n.* (slang) Either a person who gains illegal access to computer information, or a bad golfer, depending on which chips are involved. See CHIPS.

HACKNEYED, *adj.* Made trite by overuse, like ax-murder headlines.

HAIL STORM, *n.* The welcome greeting given to rain after a long dry spell.

HAIRS, *n. pl.* What judges are paid to split.

HALCYON, *adj.* The happy, tranquil days of long ago that everyone remembers, and no one recalls in any detail.

HALF DOLLAR, *n.* About the true value of what a whole dollar was worth, not so long ago.

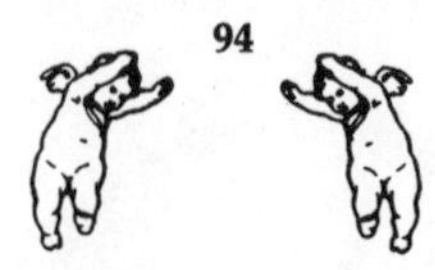

HALITOSIS, *n.* The fearful name for bad-smelling breath, a malady created by makers of mouthwashes and television commercials.

HALLOWEEN, *n.* The devilish night before All Saints' Day.

HALTER, *n.* A woman's upper garment that does not accomplish what it sounds like.

HAMLET, *n.* The title hero of a Shakespearean play, or a very small village, depending upon one's idea of tragedy.

HAPPINESS, *n.* A temporary state of affairs induced by moments of forgetfulness or of great expectations that do not materialize.

HARD-LINE, *adj.* An aggressive, non-yielding policy advocated by the hard-headed and hard-hearted against those they take to be soft-headed and soft-hearted.

Give me a policy that's truly hard-line
Whether in crime or affairs of state;
If we adhere to the toughest design
No one'll be left to negotiate.
But if we turn soft and don't draw the line,
Everyone might ponder, perhaps cogitate,
And come to agreement before it's too late.
Such an inglorious fate!

ROCKY FILE

HASTE, *n.* A rapid way of making waste, of which there is too much already.

HEAD, *n.* 1. That part of the human body reputed to house the brain, assuming the house is neither empty nor up for sale. 2. That of which two are better than one, especially if one is emptier than normal.

HEADLINES, *n. pl.* The parts of a newspaper consisting of large type for small minds.

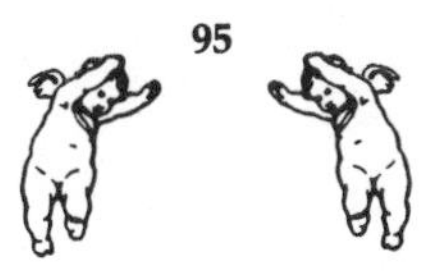

HEALTH, *n.* The usual state of body and mind until one begins to read about it or enters a doctor's office.

HEARSAY, *n.* A type of evidence, fanned in the court of public opinion, banned in a court of law.

HEART, *n.* The optimistic organ which, in circulating the blood, keeps reassuring the artery that it's not all in vein.

HEATHEN, *n.* A person happily free of sin, original or terminal.

HEAVEN, *n.* A celestial mansion, the keys to which are often lost in traveling back and forth to church.

HELL, *n.* An alluring place, known for its open doors, well-paved streets, and central heating that never breaks down.

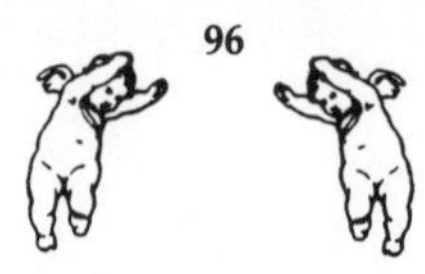

HERESY, *n.* 1. Incorrect opinions and beliefs, combated by the equally erroneous opinions and beliefs of the orthodox, particularly in religion and science. 2. A doctrine held to be false today, true tomorrow, and indifferent the day after.

HETEROSEXUAL, *n. adj.* A biological type in danger of becoming homogenized.

HIERARCHY, *n.* A rank way of organizing people in order to bring out their most offensive characteristics.

HIKE, *n.* An activity that taxes, prices, and Boy Scouts have in common, the main difference being that the scouts usually make camp instead of continuing to climb.

HINDMOST, *n.* The ones the Devil takes, whether the race is fair or not.

HIPPOCRATIC OATH, *n.* The ethical code of physicians, and presumably not subject to a second opinion.

HISTORY, *n.* A mysterious process of time that moves sideways from the present, surges forward from the past, and backward from the future.

HOLIDAY, *n.* Formerly, a day of significant religious or national meaning; now, any day that Congress or state legislatures decree as contributing to a long weekend. In the future, all persons expecting to warrant a holiday in their honor must be born on Friday or Monday.

> When Victor visited the United States, he was fascinated by all the holidays that punctuated the year. While each one had some historic meaning or purpose, he observed that for most people the main idea was time away from work. This came to his mind one New Year's Eve when he joined the throng in Times Square in New York City. Everyone was checking their watch and finally, when at midnight the huge ball on the

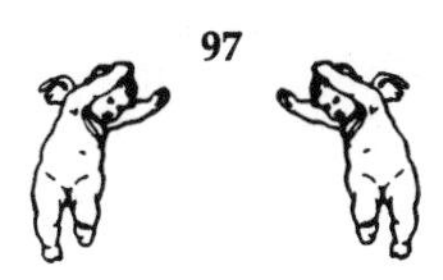

tower of the *Times* began its dramatic fall, a great roar went up from the crowd to signal the new year. "Ah," Victor murmured softly to himself, "Now it is the time off whose idea has come."

HUGO WINNER

HOLLYWOOD, *n.* An entertaining place where swimming pools are bought and wedding rings are rented.

HOMAGE, *n.* Dutiful respect, or honor.

We come to pay homage
To nuclear bombage
And its role in the balance of power;
There's no doubt about it,
We can't do without it,
Thus honoring that mushroomy flower.

NITA NOONA

HOME, *n.* A man's castle—but just in case, install a moat and keep the oil boiling.

HOMEWORK, *n.* An educational form of child labor, outlawed by professional educators as being helpful to the process of learning.

HOMO SAPIENS, *n.* (Latin) Literally, man the intelligent, a species still being sought among all those ancient bones; it is presumed to be extinct.

HONESTY, *n.* 1. A rare quality, praised in principle, despised in practice, and punished in public. 2. What is said to be the best policy, except in the advertising and insurance industries.

HONOR, *n.* That which a person has with profit in his own land or any other.

HOOKER, *n.* (slang) A prostitute or a golfer, depending on the field of play.

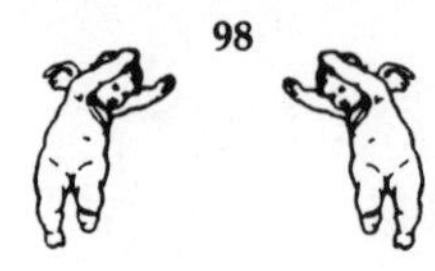

HOPE, *n.* The antidote for today's misery and the drug for tomorrow's disappointments.

HOSPITAL, *n.* A relatively benign form of military organization in which doctors are generals, nurses are foot soldiers, and patients are casualties.

HOT LINE, *n.* An urgent invention of the Cold War, designed to cool any hotheads who might be occupying the hot seats of governments.

HOUSE-HUSBAND, *n.* A newly domesticated animal replacing the housewife in the evolution of marriage.

HOUSEWIFE, *n.* An unfortunate woman who, when feeling too ill to work, can't call in sick.

HUMANITARIAN, *n.* A person so concerned with the welfare of HUMANITY, writ large, that he makes friends, writ small, miserable.

HUMOR, *n.* A feeling that comes in two varieties: good and bad, usually the latter.

HUSBAND, *n.* A man who begins as a woman's hubby, becomes her habit and, if lucky, continues as her hobby.

HYPOCRISY, *n.* The sanctimonious pretense of virtue, and therefore the most important social grace; without it others would see us as we really are, which none of us can afford.

IBID, *n.* An exotic flower in the garden of footnotes, along with such other species as *op. cit.*, and *idem.*

ICONOCLAST, *n.* A learned person who detests all forms of idiocy except his own.

ID, *n.* In Freudian theology, the id, the ego, and the superego constitute the eternal conflicting trinity of mental life.

As part of the psyche, the Id is just there;
Perhaps it is here or any old where;
Though it tries to remain hidden
It arises unbidden
Giving the Ego one hell of a scare.

BARTLEY SNOOD

IDEA, *n.* An unfamiliar object produced by thought, which is very rare, as distinguished from opinion, produced by prejudice, which is very common.

IDEAL, *n.* An idea made lofty by the simple addition of "I."

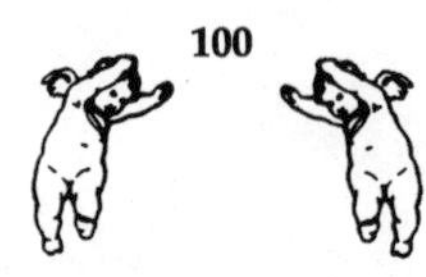

IDENTITY, *n.* The state of being of a person, which seems to be lost, since so many people are searching for one.

IDEOLOGY, *n.* The false doctrines held to be true by people known as ideologues, whose principal idols are people known as demagogues, who specialize in monologues.

IDIOT, *n.* A member of the Moronic tribe, which is always at war with the Imbeciles. Strangely, instead of killing each other off, they simply continue to multiply.

IDLENESS, *n.* A very agreeable form of inactivity, with the added virtue that it requires practically no effort to cultivate.

IGNORANCE, *n.* A blissful lack of knowledge in which people are happily instructed by the public school system. Ignorance may be no excuse in the eyes of the law, but it is very excusable in the eyes of the school.

ILLEGAL, *adj.* A category of pleasurable activities that is handy when the immoral and the fattening have been exhausted.

ILLUSTRIOUS, *adj.* Famous, outstanding; said of people who have worked industriously to foster more illusions of greatness.

IMAGINATION, *n.* A powerful creative mental force, native to children, which is so thoroughly obliterated by education that it is retained only by child-like adults known as poets, theorists, visionaries, and dreamers.

> An eighteen-month old girl, upon seeing the Pacific Ocean for the first time, said, "Big bath." That's imagination. After a few years of schooling, the same scene was merely "the ocean."

IMBROGLIO, *n.* A confused misunderstanding, often used

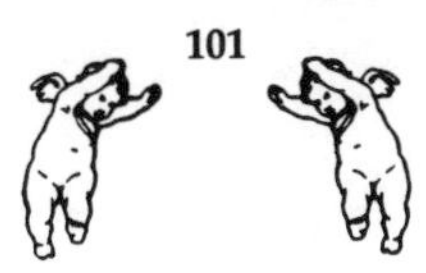

as a brief description of modern society by those who can pronounce it.

IMMOBILE, *adj.* Stable or motionless, the safest state of an automobile.

IMMORAL, *adj.* An accusation that immediately excites attention to anything the accuser deplores.

There's something attractive in what is immoral,
It deserves its own wreath, one that is floral;
So many things are honored these days,
Most of which are a passing phase.
But of this I am sure, immorality will persist
Because we all lack that will to resist—
And man will be measured
By the pleasures he's treasured.

UBIE KEANE

IMMUNOLOGY, *n.* A legal-medical specialty devoted to gaining immunity from prosecution for criminals who might otherwise suffer the dreaded diseases of conviction and punishment.

IMPARTIAL, *adj.* Fair and unbiased, a condition as impossible to imagine as it is hopeless to find.

IMPEACHMENT, *n.* A political fate that must be faced with resignation.

IMPLAUSIBLE, *adj.* Hard to believe, as, for example, the claim that a successful man was born in a shack he built himself.

IMPOLITIC, *adj.* Describing an eminently sensible but politically inexpedient course of action, recognition of which marks the difference between short and long political careers.

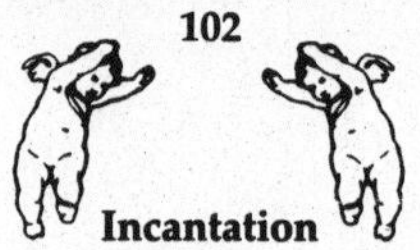

Incantation

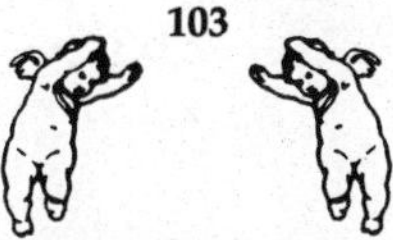

IMPOSSIBLE, *adj.* Contrary to reason; hopeless. The spirit of the word was captured perfectly by the man who discovered that no matter how long he stood in the shower he could wash away neither his fat nor his sins.

INADVERTENT, *adj.* Thoughtless or unintentional; what all mistakes are claimed to be, thus relieving the culprit of responsibility.

INCANTATION, *n.* The meaningless words or sounds used in magical spells or rites, like singing commercials or oaths of office.

INCONGRUOUS, *adj.* Unsuitable or inappropriate, like buying a cemetery plot with a view. Much that is incongruous also happens in Congress.

INCORRUPTIBLE, *adj.* Describing a momentary lack of judgment in an official who refuses the offer of a bribe, or anyone else who turns down an advantage.

INCUMBENCY, *n.* The political and financial advantage of holding office; sometimes spelled incomebuncy.

INDECENT, *adj.* Offensive to decent people—who are becoming hard to find and easy to ignore.

INDECISIVE, *adj.* Being unsure what to do in a difficult situation, which is construed by others as weakness and a lack of leadership ability. To avoid even the appearance of this, many bad decisions are made.

> In the early days of World War II, a group of new naval officers was treated to an address by a navy captain. He emphasized that naval officers would often be faced with difficult situations in which decisions would have to be made. His major advice was: "Whatever comes up, do something."

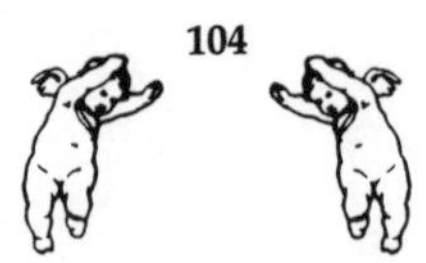

> The young officers wondered why such an old sea dog was just giving speeches instead of having a command at sea, and why he was still a captain instead of admiral. Later, it was discovered that in some naval exercises in the Pacific, the captain had run a fleet of destroyers aground. So much for "Do something."

INDIGNITY, *n.* 1. What only the indignant can suffer. 2. What many people lacking dignity claim to suffer anyway.

INDIVIDUALITY, *n.* That precious quality which is the business of education, advertising, and government to eradicate.

INDOCTRINATE, *v.* To instruct in doctrines or beliefs. This is unfortunate, unless it's for a good cause; then it is called education.

INDUSTRIALISM, *n.* A striking form of economic organization, currently characterized by capital that is inactive, labor that is lazy, and government that is very active.

INFAMOUS, *adj.* Having a bad reputation; the paradoxical description of many a famous person.

INFERENCE, *n.* A mysterious process allowing us to reach a conclusion that is desired.

> An old sea captain kept a personal diary. On his sixty-fifth birthday he wrote: "Awoke this morning with a fine erection; couldn't bend it with both hands." On his seventieth birthday he wrote: "Awoke this morning with a fine erection; couldn't bend it with both hands." On his seventy-fifth birthday he wrote: "Awoke this morning with a fine erection; could barely bend it with both hands. Must be getting stronger."
>
> PHINEAS PLONK

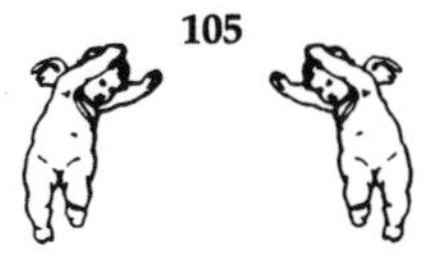

INFINITIVE, *n.* A verb form that is often deliberately split to gain clarity of meaning, at the risk of reprimand by those purists who would rather be formally artificial than articulately functional.

INFLATION, *n.* A chronic illness of modern economies, the symptoms of which are a rise in prices and a decline in value.

INFRANGIBLE, *adj.* Fortunately, a word that is never remembered, rarely used, and can always be looked up in dire circumstance of need.

INHERITANCE, *n.* The taxes that weren't collected when living.

INHIBITIONS, *n. pl.* The things that are gained in prohibitions and shed in exhibitions.

INHUMAN, *adj.* Heartless, cruel, brutal—the normal, if paradoxical, word for describing the human condition.

INITIATIVE, *n.* 1. That which one should take before losing it. 2. In democracies, the generally unwelcome idea that citizens have a right to propose and vote on legislation designed to remedy the evils inflicted upon them by the sins of omission or commission of their elected representatives.

INJUSTICE, *n.* The inevitable result of a legal system devoted more to praising justice than practicing it.

INNOCENCE, *n.* A quality of life that, once lost, is never regained.

INNUENDO, *n.* A derogatory insinuation, the essence of gossip, the life-blood of journalism, the heart of politics.

INQUISITION, *n.* A religious tribunal of terror, the rehearsal for modern press conferences, congressional hearings, and audits by the Internal Revenue Service.

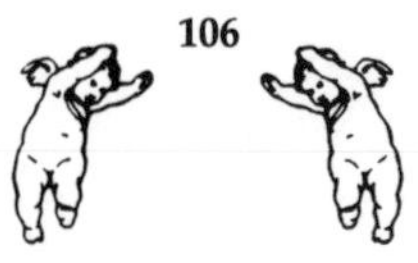

INSANITY, *n.* A mental condition, problematical in medicine, but so fully understood in law as to justify verdicts of not guilty by virtue of it.

INSENSITIVITY, *n.* A severely damaging charge leveled against any public figure who does not share the same social and political allergies as the accusers.

INSIGHT, *n.* The sudden, inspired understanding that is rich in hindsight, poor in foresight.

INTEGRITY, *n.* My unswerving devotion to principle, as distinguished from your unyielding inflexibility, known as stubbornness.

INTELLECTUAL, *n.* A person whose intellect improves much faster than his income.

INTELLIGENT LIFE, *n.* That which is being sought on other planets, which is understandable in light of its short supply on this one.

INTEREST RATES, *n. pl.* The cost of borrowing money. Rates rise and fall at the whim of bankers whose primary interest is in charging the most for the least.

The rate of interest in interest rates
Rises fast and then abates,
   As interest wanes
   In others' gains
To rise again with Watergates.

Sterling Swoop

INTOLERANCE, *n.* A prejudicial attitude the intolerant attribute to those others of a different persuasion.

IRRATIONAL, *adj.* Describing the beliefs, statements, or actions of people we refuse to understand, as opposed to rational, which describes those who agree with us.

JAWBONE, *v.* A modern political activity, borrowed from the Bible, whereby one ass, who is in authority, tries to persuade another ass, who is not, to be even more of one.

JEALOUSY, *n.* A wholesome emotion that stimulates rivalry, animates romance, and saves marriages.

JEANS, *n. pl.* A garment designed in accord with the principle that the jeans justify the ends in view.

JESUIT, *n.* A member of a religious order renowned for its sophistication as much as its sophistry.

JET SET, *n.* A modern version of the leisure class, the members of which fly together chic to chic.

JINGOISM, *n.* An abnormal advocacy of a war-like foreign policy, as distinguished from patriotism, which requires only the normal amount of same.

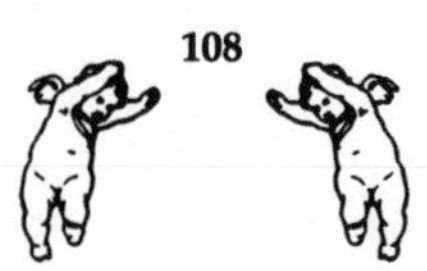

JOGGING, *n.* An esoteric type of running composed of one part physical exercise, two parts talking about it, and three parts medical mysticism.

If old age you wish to see
Neither a jogger nor a joiner be;
Both in their respective ways
Evoke much credit, even praise,
But in the end it's just a craze.

The joiner died, alone in his bed,
The jogger while still in his shoes;
Sad it was, but everyone said
"Whatever else, they paid their dues."

CLAUDE CLECKEM

JOKE, *n.* Something to laugh at, unless it's practically played on you.

JONAH, *n.* The hero of one of the Biblical fish tales, who lived at a time when it was more fashionable to save people than whales.

JOURNALIST, *n.* A person who, mistaking his prejudices for news, accordingly collects, selects, and presents the latter to correspond with the former.

JUDGE, *n.* 1. A formerly unremarkable person who, upon elevation to the bench, immediately becomes "Your Honor," in order that all his past and future transgressions will be treated with proper respect. 2. A robed figure with regal bearing, empowered to instruct a jury without enlightening it, and to order it to ignore everything it has just learned.

JUDICIARY, *n.* The most powerful branch of government; it administers justice according to the dim lights of the law and the prevailing standards of blindness.

JUG, *n.* A little brown container, loved in song and story for its spiritual contents.

Jogging

JUNGLE, *n.* In modern usage, a term for those urban centers where the rat race is run by real rats.

JURISPRUDENCE, *n.* A philosophical branch of law, the duty of which is to provide convincing rationalizations for legal doctrines that otherwise would rightly be regarded as absurd.

JURIST, *n.* One who writes with certainty about the uncertainties of the law as if they were readily ascertainable.

JURY, *n.* A group of people so bewildered by the evidence and the rules of law that a truer verdict could be reached by a flip of the coin.

A jury of peers
Hears evidence
But what it hears
May make no sense,
For lawyer's words
Are thick and dense,
Witnesses
Are very tense
Dreading questions
In suspense,
As prosecution
Ties defense
And truth departs
Who knows whence?

OPIE GRUNT

JUSTICE, *n.* The arbitrary resolution of a troublesome situation by those who happen to be in power. It comes in three varieties—legal, social, and economic—none of which acknowledges kinship with the others. Unlike beauty or obscenity, which are in the eye of the beholder, justice is found in the eye of the beholden.

KEYNOTE, *n.* The first major speech at political conventions, intended to give life to the party.

KICK, *n.* What, in business, one gets upstairs with, when things downstairs aren't going so well.

KILL, *v.* What editors do to stories that are either too weak or too strong for their taste.

KILLING, *n.* 1. That which is easier to make in a meat market than in the stock market. 2. What hired gunmen make for a living.

KINDERGARTEN, *n.* An early form of education wherein children are taught how to behave in school without learning anything.

KINDRED, *n.* The uneasy feeling that arises when relatives come for a visit.

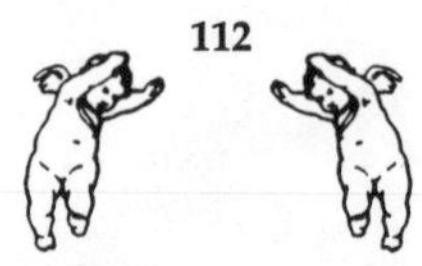

KINGS, *n. pl.* Sovereigns who were once believed to have a divine right to govern. Then God changed his mind and gave that right to the people, along with the divine right to be wrong.

KITCHENWARE, *n.* An apron and a chef's hat are considered appropriate.

KLEPTOMANIA, *n.* The overwhelming impulse to steal, an occupational disease of bankers, politicians, and tax agents.

KNEE-JERK, *adj.* In modern political rhetoric, an unthinking response to the ills of society. Once the monopoly of bleeding-heart liberals, it is now possessed by hard-hearted conservatives, who are just as unthinking.

KNOT, *n.* A bond that is tied in matrimony, tightened in parenthood, and untied in divorce.

KNOW-HOW, *n.* A widely praised American trait that carefully avoids such unimportant items as "Know what" or "Know why." "Know who" is still permitted.

KNOWLEDGE, *n.* A profound form of understanding, equally and mercifully denied to both the know-it-alls and the know-nothings.

KREMLIN, *n.* The collective name for the White House, Congress, Supreme Court, and Pentagon of the Soviet Union—and it speaks with one voice.

KREMLINOLOGY, *n.* The learned attempt to understand the behavior of the Kremlin, and about as successful as criminology.

KU KLUX KLAN, *n.* An organization devoted to wearing white sheets and masks while displaying its preference for ignorance and prejudice.

LABORATORY, *n.* 1. The experimental Cathedral of a modern religion called Science, based on Priestly traditions; often pronounced Labo-Rat-ory. 2. A very unsafe place for animals.

LABOR OF LOVE, *n.* The extraordinary effort put forth by women, nine months later.

LABOR-SAVING DEVICE, *n.* Either a successful form of contraception or an abortion, whichever comes first.

LABOR UNION, *n.* An organization that organizes workers in order to obtain many benefits, including striking, walking picket lines, and those that accrue to the leaders.

LAISSEZ-FAIRE, *n.* A traditional doctrine of capitalism, under which private industry and business are to be let alone by government, so that the invisible hand can give the unsuspecting a finger.

There's little fair in Laissez-Faire,
And truth is not at stake;

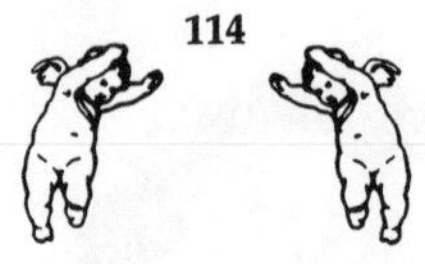

What concerns the doctrinaire
Are questions of a different air:
How much profit will it make,
How much cheating will it take?

HARVEY GLUG

LAME DUCK, *n.* A politician one step removed from being a dead duck.

LANDLADY, *n.* A suspicious woman who keeps a respectable house, whether a landlord is home or not.

LANGUAGE, *n.* A set of symbols people use to communicate with each other, usually without much success.

LARCENY, *n.* Theft—a little of it is in the heart of everyone, and a lot of it is on the mind of most.

LAUGHING STOCK, *n.* An excellent investment, occasionally found on Wall Street, that tickles the money bone; as opposed to Crying Stock, so prevalent on Wail Street, where losers weep.

LAUGHTER, *n.* 1. That which, together with lying and literature, most distinctively separates man from other forms of wild life. 2. The sound that charlatans and fools fear most.

LAUNCHING PAD, *n.* A modern apartment where, through the magic of chemistry, space trips can be taken without the inconvenience of leaving home.

LAURELS, *n. pl.* As good a place to rest on as any, and better than most.

LAWS, *n. pl.* The infernal things constantly being passed by pernicious legislators laboring under the delusion that if some laws are good, more are better. Unneeded by the virtuous, and unheeded by the wicked, their main effect is to harass the citizenry, enrich the lawyers, and clog the courts with senseless litigation.

When men make laws, it gives us pause,
And something else to do—
Thoughts of breaking unjust laws
And who is there to sue?
Then come the snarls and legal quarrels,
And public ballyhoo,
About the cops, about the courts,
And things that lawyers do.
With all the crimes and civil torts,
Disagreements of all sorts
(As to sin and who has warts),
We must await the next reports
From all the courts of last resorts.

DUMBLE B. SPREE

LAWSUIT, *n.* The most expensive part of an attorney's wardrobe, used for appearances in courts and banks.

LAWYER, *n.* A person professionally trained in the difference between a jury and perjury, and skilled in the art of using both to best advantage.

LAWYERS, *n. pl.* In a nation that falsely prides itself on living "under the rule of law," lawyers are the most powerful class. As legislators, they write the laws badly; as judges, they interpret laws whimsically; and as attorneys they are paid to evade the same laws in practice. Since all of this is adverse to the well-being of ordinary citizens, our legal system is rightly described as being adversarial in character.

LECTURE, *n.* A lengthy scolding students must endure in lecture halls.

LEFT WINGER, *n.* An extreme liberal who claims his heart is in the right place, even if his head always isn't; as distinguished from a right-winger, who is an extreme conserva-

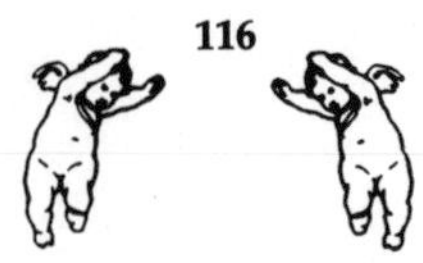

tive and claims that his head is in the right place even if his heart always isn't. Neither will admit they don't know where the right place is.

LEGAL TENDER, *n.* A touching love affair with money.

LEGISLATOR, *n.* 1. An elected official who would rather pass a bad law than none at all. 2. A law-maker who has never learned that the more he makes, the more will be broken—and that repairs are costly.

LEISURE, *n.* A worthy form of idleness that must be worked at with diligence and dignity if its full worth is to be realized.

LIBERAL ARTS, *n. pl.* Those nonutilitarian courses of study that liberate the mind and enslave the conscience.

LIBERTINE, *n.* A person who wants to take liberties without losing any.

LIBERTY, *n.* Freedom—it is praised in speech, feared in practice, because such a narrow line separates use from abuse.

LICENSE, *n.* A piece of paper required for practically all the important activities of life, except birth and death, when a certificate must suffice.

LIE, *n.* The opposite of the whole truth; a twin to the half-truth.

LIFE, *n.* 1. An endurance contest among pain, pleasure, and boredom. With the increase in life expectancy, the third keeps pulling ahead. 2. That which begins when the children move out and the pets die away.

LINE, *n.* The thing that must be drawn somewhere, not just anywhere, if it is to be held firmly.

LITERACY, *n.* The unfortunate disability of people who still read and write in an age of television, statistics, and computers.

LITIGANT, *n.* A party to a law suit, to which lawyers extend the invitations, and a judge acts as host.

LIVER, *n.* An organ of certain animals which, after a lifetime of secreting bile and metabolizing who knows what, is still regarded as an edible delicacy by people of extremely dubious taste.

LOBBY, *n.* An ornate lounge, with stuffed chairs, in which persons with stuffed wallets, called lobbyists, bribe stuffed animals, called politicians, with the intent of stuffing further those same wallets by unstuffing the citizens, called taxpayers.

LOGIC, *n.* Any mode of reasoning, or reasonable facsimile thereof, that permits one to reach the desired conclusion.

Logic is a little game
Played in arguments;
Your points are all so tame
While mine are full of sense.
In the end, it's all the same:
One person's logic
Is another's inference.

NORVAL NICELY

LONELINESS, *n.* The dark shadow of the bright side of solitude.

LONG DISTANCE, *n.* The best type of communication since it keeps the talkers at least at arm's length.

LONGITUDE, *n.* A distance on the map that gives considerable latitude to the prime meridian, whatever that may be.

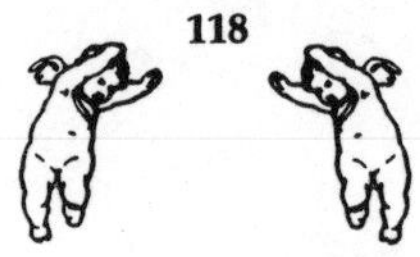

LONG-SUFFERING, *adj.* The long-standing, listening to the long-winded.

LOQUACIOUS, *adj.* Very talkative; what liquor adds to the vivacious.

LOVE MATCH, *n.* A romantic relationship that begins with a flame and ends in a burn.

LUCK, *n.* Chance or fortune. It comes in two varieties: good and bad. The latter is always recognized for what it is; the former is usually mistaken for skill, effort, ability, and the like.

Luck may be a lady
Who's either bad or good;
I'd like to know her better
And woo her if I could,
Scorning her when bad,
Embracing when she's good.

HI ROLLER

LURID, *adj.* Shocking or sensational, such as the "crime of the century," which is reported several times a week, each one being different.

LUXURIES, *n. pl.* The unnecessary, costly things we become so accustomed to that they become necessities.

LYING, *n.* The first resort of the guilty, which is why it is so common.

LYRICIST, *n.* A person whose words can face the music, as distinguished from a composer, whose music can pace the words.

MACE, *n.* Traditionally, a solid symbol of authority; now, a gaseous substance also symbolizing authority.

MAD, *n.* The acronym for "mutually assured destruction," the official nuclear policy of the United States and the Soviet Union. Not coincidentally, the word also means insane, delusionary, and irrational—making it probably the most accurate acronym ever devised.

MADISON AVENUE, *n.* The Dream Street of hucksters where consumers are lulled to sleep.

MAFIA, *n.* A society of criminals, so secret that its members are known to everyone but law enforcement officials.

MAGNETIC POLE, *n.* A charming, attractive native of Poland.

MAIDEN SPEECH, *n.* A verbal gambit which, if successful, is given only once to the same audience.

MANAGER, *n.* 1. In baseball, a person whose profound

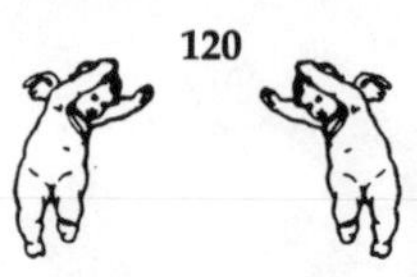

knowledge of the game keeps him from confusing a double play with a double-header; and who spells relief with a pitcher rather than a catcher. 2. The leader of a baseball team, which needs coaching, as distinguished from a coach, who leads a football team that needs managing.

MAN IN THE STREET, *n.* The "average person," as viewed by anyone who considers himself above the crowd.

MANY, *n., adj.* A multiple sexist word that has been condemned by feminists and their sympathizers, who wish the Bible to read: "A large number are called but few are chosen."

MARDI GRAS, *n.* An ecstatic, annual religious festival at which all celebrants possess a devout license to sin.

MARRIAGE, *n.* A legal union of husband and wife, the members of which pay dues in return for the right to strike—each other.

MARTINI, *n.* The great tranquilizer, inspired and required by the stresses of modern civilization. See also COLD COMFORT.

MARTYR, *n.* A person with the foresight to suffer and die for an unpopular cause, but only if it later becomes legitimate.

MASS COMMUNICATION, *n.* A collective phrase designating all those modern media devoted so exclusively to keeping the masses "masses."

MAXIM, *n.* A short, verbal rule of conduct, as distinguished from maximum, which is either a long silence or a long sentence.

MAY DAY, *n.* The internationally recognized sign of distress, perhaps because it follows the cruelest month.

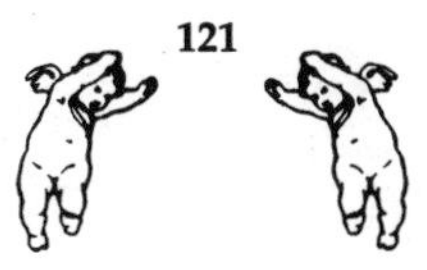

"April is the cruellest month,"
So T. S. Eliot wrote,
But were the matter put to test,
May would get my vote.

The cruel and distressing
Are alike in many ways,
When all is said and done;
April has but thirty days
While May has thirty-one,
And thus distress is given
A longer course to run.

SETH GRIMBY

MAYFLOWER COMPACT, *n.* A patriotic cosmetic kit designed for the Daughters of the American Revolution.

MC CARTHYISM, *n.* A species of political persecution which, for a few years, proved that guilt by association and accusation were more powerful than guilt by adjudication.

MEA CULPA, *n.* A Latin phrase meaning admission of fault or blame by the speaker; very rare, either in Latin or English, and never in journalese.

MEANINGFUL, *adj.* A textbook case of how a once reasonable term can be so abused as to become meaning-empty, as in a "meaningful relationship," or a "meaningful remedy" as in law. See REMEDY.

MEASURE, *n.* That which one should carefully take of another before picking a fight or trying to measure up.

MEDICATION, *n.* An extravagant word for medicine, lavishly prescribed by physicians for the enrichment of drug companies and pharmacists.

MEDICINE SHOW, *n.* A tedious entertainment put on by the Food and Drug Administration, and "public interest"

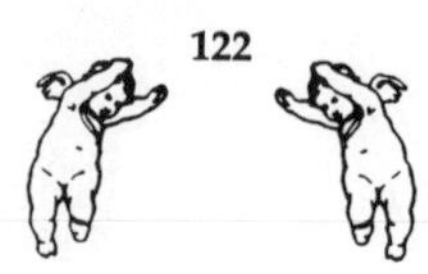

groups who can always spot a potential risk in anything that conceivably might benefit the sick. A not untypical statement would read like this: "Some scientists believe this product has a potential of possibly creating hazards to populations capable of being at risk."

MEEK, *n.* The people who will inherit the earth after the real estate has been sufficiently ravaged by the strong.

MEMORY, *n.* A mysterious property of the mind that works best when it is equally selective about what to recall and what to forget.

MENTAL HEALTH, *n.* The priceless possession of a few who are able to display serenity in the insane world of the many; probably illusory.

MENTAL ILLNESS, *n.* An affliction of those who seem to march to a drummer unheard by, or unknown to, the rest of us—each of whom has his own drummer.

MERCY DEATH, *n.* An act so sensible and humane that it naturally creates all kinds of ethical problems and is forbidden by law. If there is to be any legitimate killing it must be the merciless kind of the state, called capital punishment.

MICROLOGY, *n.* The elaborate discussion of trivial affairs, best exemplified by television talk shows, political pundits, and the *Congressional Record.*

MICROSCOPE, *n.* An instrument that magnifies, thus making small things look large, such as political campaigns. In that sense television is the electronic microscope of society.

MIND, *n.*, *v.* 1. The thinking apparatus that it is better to get things off of before you go out of it. 2. What one should do with his or her own business.

MINSTREL SHOW, *n.* The late, meretricious, and unlamented travesty on black humor.

MINUTES, *n. pl.* The official fabrication of the last meeting; always approved, not because they are accurate, but because they are accomplished.

MIRACLE DRUG, *n.* A religious opiate said to cure the doubts of the faithfully ill.

MIRAGE, *n.* An optical illusion, resembling a miracle, such as a balanced federal budget or an impartial inquiry.

MISAPPREHENSION, *n.* A wrong idea, most of which are apprehended only too well by all too many.

MISCREATE, *v.* To form unnaturally, which, since it happened at the beginning, accounts for a world full of miscreants.

MISDATE, *n.* The beginning of a very short courtship.

MISER, *n.* A person with the good sense to value money above all other things; people lacking this sense are called miserable.

MISFORTUNE, *n.* Bad luck not of one's own fault, such as being born, called for jury duty, drafted into the armed forces, and similar adversities.

MISGIVING, *n.* The uneasy feeling that arises when asked to contribute to a worthy cause.

MISGOVERNMENT, *n.* 1. Bad government or management, the permanent state of public affairs. 2. A chronic illness of modern society, the symptoms of which are so ubiquitous they are accepted as normal.

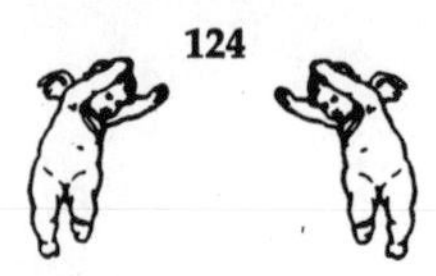

MISHMASH, *n.* A confused mixture, like a party platform, a Supreme Court decision, or a resolution of the United Nations.

MISINFORMATION, *n.* That which is known as "news" among journalists, commentators, investigative reporters, and the like, who, in accord with natural law, have evolved from a hunting and gathering stage of news to the manufacture thereof.

MISMATCH, *n.* An unequal contest between unsuitable opponents, as in a marriage.

MISS, *n.* An unmarried lady, from whence comes the saying "A miss is as good as a smile."

MISSAL, *n.* A prayer book, handy to have in church or other dangerous places. The Catholic version was known as the first intercontinental missal.

MIXED MARRIAGE, *n.* Traditionally, one in which the two partners came from different racial, religious, or ethnic backgrounds. Today it also applies to those marriages where the partners are of different sexes.

MNEMONIC, *adj.* Intended to aid the memory—a word singularly ill-equipped for the task.

MODELING, *n.* What economists do for the economy, and others do for a living; the latter have more success but the former have more power.

MODERN, *adj.* Describing anything that has had time enough to become modish but not enough time to become outmoded, when it becomes traditional.

MODEST, *adj.* Humble, or lacking vanity. Winston Churchill, not known for his own modesty, once described a contemporary as "a modest man—and indeed he has much

125

Mixed Marriage

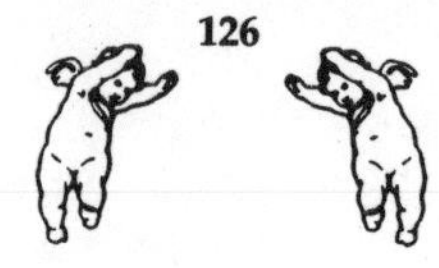

to be modest about." Still, at least a modicum of modesty is regarded as becoming.

MODERATOR, *n.* A presiding officer, chosen for being more moderate than the orators he moderates.

MODUS OPERANDI, *n.* (Latin) A method of working, which has the unfortunate habit of interfering with one's modus vivendi.

MOMENTUM, *n.* An almost mystical impetus that political campaigns or athletic teams momentarily acquire or lose, according to the momentous commentary of breathless reporters.

MONARCHY, *n.* A hereditary form of government in which the throne is maintained by putting on heirs.

MONEY, *n.* The green stuff that talks loud, unless it is thrown by governments at big problems, when it becomes a whisper of its former self.

MONOGAMY, *n.* A form of marriage characterized by monotony.

MONOGRAPH, *n.* A scholarly study of a narrow, technical subject, written to be read by a narrow, technical audience, but usually isn't. Even so, one's autograph on a monograph is useful for self-promotion and tenure.

MONOMANIA, *n.* An abnormal, obsessive interest in, and concern with, a single subject or idea, the major form of which is egomania.

MONOTHEIST, *n.* A brave, idealistic person willing to believe in only one God, as distinguished from a polytheist, who is a more practical person and believes in many Gods—just in case there is safety in numbers.

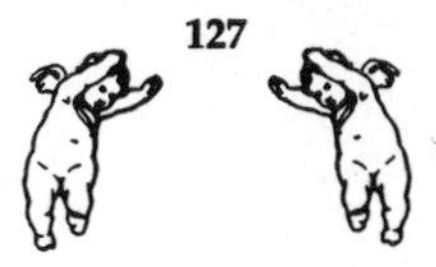

MONUMENTS, *n. pl.* Lifeless tributes, in steel, concrete, and marble, to dead heroes and forgotten events.

MORAL, *adj.* A term describing anything I think good, without knowing the reasons thereof, as opposed to immoral, which is anything I think bad, also without knowing the reasons. ("What is moral is what you feel good after and what is immoral is what you feel bad after."—E. Hemingway.)

MORALIST, *n.* A person who teaches, studies, or writes about morals in lieu of practicing them.

MORAL VICTORY, *n.* What one claims to have won in the face of an obvious defeat, and for which, therefore, moral support is sought.

MORE, *adj.* What people more or less want more of.

MORNING AFTER, *n.* The one that greets a day of reckoning.

MORTALITY, *n.* The end that treats the moral and the immoral with equal indifference.

MOTHER'S DAY, *n.* An annual commercial and sentimental event, dedicated more to money than maternity.

MOTORCADE, *n.* A procession of automobiles, signaling that something unpleasant is going on, such as a funeral or the arrival of politicians and diplomats.

MOUNTAINS, *n. pl.* What headlines make out of molehills in the land of journalism.

MOUSETRAP, *n.* An object you have to make a better one of if, for some perverse reason, you wish to have the world beat at your door.

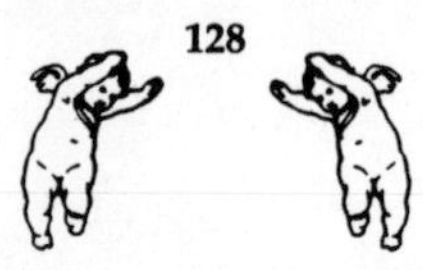

MOUTH, *n.* A dangerous part of the anatomy, especially if it is big, loud, and shoots off a lot.

MUCKRAKING, *n.* The forerunner of "investigative reporting," in that both involve journalists who seek and expose corruption wherever it can be found. A conspicuous exception are the media themselves which presumably lack the proper rake for all the muck there.

MUDDLE THROUGH, *v.* To produce bungling and confusion—brought to its highest peak of perfection by military organizations and police departments the world over.

MUDSLINGING, *n.* The first desperate resort of political opponents.

MULE, *n.* An animal resembling a horse, best known for its stamina, stubbornness, and sterility.

MULTIDISCIPLINARY, *adj.* Involving many branches of learning, a type of research that Mr. Justice Frankfurter once characterized as "the cross-sterilization of knowledge."

MULTIFARIOUS, *adj.* Many and various, a description of nefarious schemes.

MULTINATIONAL CORPORATIONS, *n. pl.* Economic empires that are supra-national, verging on the supernatural, above and beyond earthly control.

MUSES, *n. pl.* The nine Greek goddesses who were the inspiration for art and science, of which the two most interesting were Amuse and Bemuse.

MUSHROOM, *n.* An edible fungus that makes a gorgeous soup and casts a giant cloud over the world.

MUSTARD, *n.* The substance one must be able to cut to prove how sharp he or she is.

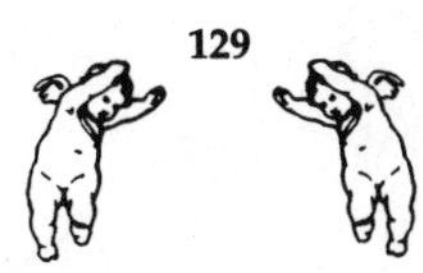

MUSTER, *n.* A curious point one must pass in order to come up to the standards of someone else.

MYOPIA, *n.* The short-sightedness of man that obscures the vision of utopia.

MYTH, *n.* An erroneous belief which, when recognized as such, is immediately replaced by another, since error knows no limits.

NAIL, *n.* An object that is occasionally hit on the head, just as a blind hog will sometimes find an acorn.

NARROW, *adj.* The normal range of the human mind after it has been exposed to parents, teachers, and other adults.

NATIONALISM, *n.* A pride of country, which becomes the bride of nationalistic ambition, and the mother of war.

NATIONAL SECURITY, *n.* A concept similar to national defense, but much more general and mysterious in character. Its principal function is to guard the insecurities of the administration in power, which can be very general and mysterious indeed.

NATION-STATE, *n.* A modern political entity whose main interest in its citizens is governed by the "shut" principle: shut in, shut out, shut up, shut down, and shut off.

NAUTICAL, *adj.* Describing the sometimes boisterous behavior of sailors on shore leave.

NAUTS, *n. pl.* (slang) Americans call them Astro, Russians call them Cosmo—in either case they're pretty far out.

NECESSARY EVIL, *n.* An unpleasantness that cannot be avoided, according to people who are up to no good.

NECK, *n.* 1. A part of the human anatomy one should be careful about sticking out unless prepared to have it cut off. 2. A part of the anatomy that does not receive much attention until discovered by adolescents in the back seat of an automobile.

NEEDLE, *n.* A small, funny-shaped object, with an eye at one end and a sharp point at the other. The latter is used to annoy people, the former to test the religious mobility of camels.

NE'ER-DO-WELL, *n.* An irresponsible person with the great virtue of ne'er-doing-ill either.

NEGOTIATIONS, *n. pl.* A process of give-and-take, in which both sides, in good faith, try to take more than they give—until one side gives in, and the other takes out. In this way a reluctant agreement is reached, with both sides claiming victory.

NEIGHBORHOOD, *n.* The local thug.

NEIGHBORS, *n. pl.* People who know enough about each other to build fences and lock the doors.

The Smiths and Jones
Lived side by side
With many bones to pick;
They used the phones,
They pried and spied,
Their tempers at the quick.
For many years
This thing remained

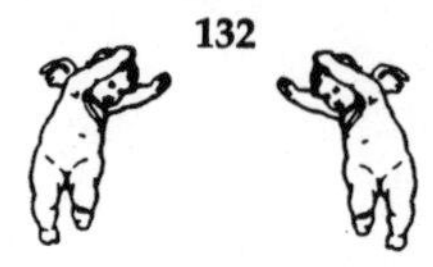

Before the conflict ceased.
Wisdom they had gained:
"That neighbor neighbors
Best who neighbors least."

J. ODELL BLEAK

NEOLIBERALISM, *n.* The old liberalism that has changed its name without altering its character, as contrasted with neoconservatism which has altered its name without changing its character.

NEOLOGISM, *n.* The coining of new words that are unnecessary; the art of making new words do old tricks.

NEOPHYTE, *n.* A new convert, i.e., a person who decided to switch rather than fight.

NEPOTISM, *n.* The despicable practice of gaining revenge on society by placing one's relatives in important positions.

NET, *n.* The object dividing a tennis court, being always higher on your side than on your opponent's side.

NET NATIONAL PRODUCT, *n.* In economics, the fictional number left after all fabricated deductions have been taken from the equally fictional gross national product.

NETWORKS, *n. pl.* Monsters of television, fed by ratings in order to produce pygmies of programs.

NEUROTIC, *adj.* Suffering from some form of anxiety or emotional instability, each person in his or her own way. In current usage, it is perfectly permissible to describe someone as being normally neurotic, or neurotically normal.

NEUTRON BOMB, *n.* A particularly thoughtful and ingenious weapon, capable of killing people without the inconvenience of destroying property.

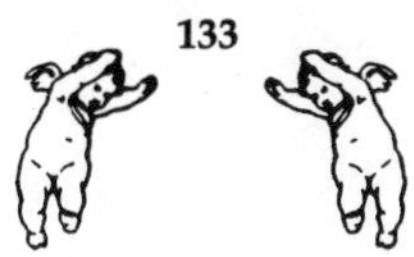

NEW DEAL, *n.* A political card game, devised in the 1930s, wherein all the players were dealt a hand, with the trumps and tricks remaining in the hand of the government.

NEWS, *n.* Today's events, reported tonight, to be forgotten tomorrow.

NIGHT, *n.* The period of darkness between sunset and sunrise. We are also in the dark as to why, if it is night that falls, it is day that breaks.

NINETEENTH HOLE, *n.* The one in golf that makes the previous eighteen bearable.

NO, *adv.* Negative; a word that, if used more often by everyone, would have many positive results.

NO-ACCOUNT, *adj., n.* (slang) Worthless; one lacking a bank account or who is overdrawn.

NOBEL PEACE PRIZE, *n.* The one awarded for promoting international peace—a gesture which almost invariably generates much international controversy, which is neither noble nor peaceful.

NOBLESSE OBLIGE, *n.* (French) The foolish belief that important people undertake many unpleasant tasks out of a sense of obligation, whereas, in truth, many unpleasant people do a lot of foolish things without any sense at all.

NO-CONFIDENCE, *n.* A political judgment which, in the United States, must await expression at the next election, by which time it is too late to do any good.

NO FAULT, *adj.* A humane form of modern permissiveness, in which legal blame is not assigned to anyone in such trivial matters as traffic accidents and divorces, so long as someone pays.

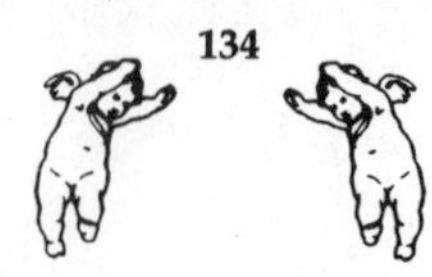

NOISE, *n.* A pervasive pollutant of modern life, particularly offensive to the ear and the sublime silence of thought.

NOLO CONTENDERE (Latin) A legal phrase meaning that the contender felt innocent enough to hire a defense attorney, but guilty enough not to fight the charge.

NOMAD, *n.* A peaceful member of a wandering tribe, until members of other tribes are encountered, whereupon he can become very mad indeed.

NOM DE PLUME, *n.* (French) A name assumed by a writer to avoid personal attack by a critic, known as a Nom De Guerre.

NOMENCLATURE, *n.* A system of technical words used by members of particular professions or occupations to baffle outsiders; a pretentious term for jargon.

NOMINATE, *v.* To place a person's name in contention for election with the expectation that the one who nominated will be properly compensated.

NONAGGRESSION, *adj.* Specifying no aggressive action, as in a nonaggression pact, which is the time to double the guard and train the troops.

NONCOMBATANTS, *n. pl.* 1. The civilian casualties of modern warfare, or any other kind for that matter. 2. A technical military term designating people who are not supposed to kill or be killed—but if it happens, what the hell.

NONEVENT, *n.* A happening that did not happen, contrary to expectations that it would happen, thus producing a news item of considerable importance.

NONPROFIT, *adj.* A profitable way of describing organizations that have successfully outwitted the Internal Revenue Service to become tax-exempt. To further the cause, contributions to such organizations then become tax-deductible, and everyone profits.

NOOSE, *n.* The way "news" is spelled during a trial that is tried more in the media than in the courts; the only remaining legitimate type of public lynching.

NORMAL, *adj.* 1. That which is usual. This underlines a paradox of modern life where the unusual is more normal than the usual, and the abnormal is celebrated. 2. Average in intelligence, which tells us more about our ignorance of intelligence than about the intelligence of the average.

NOSE, *n.* A sense organ useful for breathing and smelling. Since the former is necessary, and necessarily entails the latter, one has to take the good with the bad. The nose also has the unfortunate propensity of being stuck into other people's business with a fair chance of winding up out of joint.

NOSTALGIA, *n.* A romantic longing for a time or event recalled only in one's imagination.

NOTABLE, *adj.* Worthy of notice; conspicuous.

Some people want to be notable
In hopes of becoming more votable;
But, quick as a flash,
Recall Ogden Nash,
Who eschewed being votable,
But still was quite notable,
By being so devilishly quotable.

MINER TWINER

NOTARY PUBLIC, *n.* A stranger who certifies that you are who you claim to be.

NOTHING, *n.* A thing that does not exist, casting doubt on the statement that "Nothing succeeds like success."

NOUVEAUX RICHES, *n. pl.* (French) A disparaging phrase applied to those shameless enough to make a lot of money without the benefit of proper social standing. Old money fears new money until sanctified by a proper marriage.

NUCLEAR FREEZE, *n.* A military policy now advocated to thwart the arrival of a nuclear winter, thus providing another index to the semantic confusions of our time.

NUCLEAR WINTER, *n.* A one-time spectacular season, following upon the fall of nuclear warheads, and preceding the most silent spring on record.

NUDITY, *n.* Nakedness, especially of the human body, now so thoroughly exposed that it barely raises an eyebrow.

NUISANCE, *n.* Anything or anyone that is disagreeable or annoying. A public nuisance is one who appears too often in the news or on television.

NUMISMATICS, *n.* The study or collecting of coins, paper money, etc.; a perfectly harmless hobby unless it is yours that are being studied for the purpose of being collected.

NURSERY, *n.* A place where children and other young plants are raised for later resettlement.

NYMPH, *n.* A lovely young lady whom it is not desirable for a man to develop a mania for.

OATH, *n.* Either a sacred declaration to speak the truth, or a profane curse, depending upon whether one is a witness in court, or an eyewitness to life.

OBEDIENCE, *n.* The first requisite of citizenship and slavery, the last one for liberty and conscience.

OBESITY, *n.* The condition of being very fat. In the *Index Medicus,* the entry for obesity is followed immediately by obituary, a sequence that may not be entirely accidental.

OBFUSCATION, *n.* A marvelous word meaning confusion and bewilderment, which it is the chief business of law and philosophy to promote in as muddled a manner as is reasonably possible.

OBJECTIVITY, *n.* Subjectivity, expressed statistically.

OBSCENE, *adj.,* OBSCENITY, *n.* Both words derive from the Latin, meaning things that should be "off stage," or not exposed to public view. Somewhat myopically, history has tended to identify this solely with matters sexual and erotic

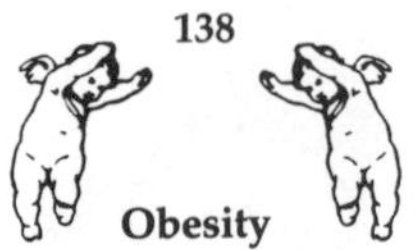

Obesity

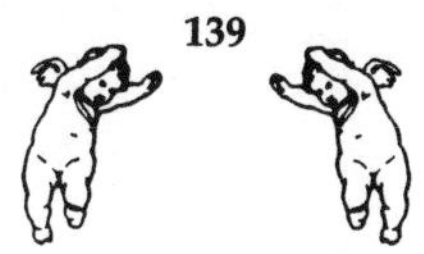

whereas, in truth, many other things qualify; such as vivid portrayals of senseless violence and detailed accounts of presidential surgery.

> A Supreme Court Justice is reported to have said that while he can't define obscenity, he knows it when he sees it. The only proper response is that there are many more things obscene than are seen in his philosophy.

OBSERVATORY, *n.* An expensive installation, expensively equipped, that tells us more about the stars than we care to know, and nothing about the earth, of which we care a lot. On second thought, perhaps it is safer to observe the stars, wherein our destiny lies not, than to observe ourselves wherein our destiny may truly lie.

O. D., *n.* (slang) Overdose, usually of a narcotic, that frequently renders one DOA, Dead On Arrival.

ODDS AND ENDS, *n. pl.* The losing tickets that litter the race track grounds.

ODOMETER, *n.* An automotive instrument which, in many used car lots, is subject to change without notice.

OFF-COLOR, *adj.* What a color television set and its programs usually are.

OIL, *n.* A very valuable resource, useful in greasing palms.

OLD AGE, *n.* A time of life when the phone rings less often, but more ominously.

OLD-FASHIONED, *adj., n.* 1. Suited to past times, which is to say, out of fashion. 2. An alcoholic drink that is never out of fashion.

OLD MAID, *n.* One who aged successfully without the interference of a husband.

OLYMPIAD, *n.* An assembly, every four years, of gifted athletes from all over the world, trained to compete in an infinity of athletic contests that seem to go on without end. Intended to promote international peace and understanding, it consistently degenerates into the most virulent nationalism this side of war, which it is coming to resemble. Nations have forbidden their athletes to participate, solely because of international conflict, and recent sites of the games have been the scenes of massacre and security measures that would be appropriate for the most secret military bases. The athletes are civilian-soldiers, marching to the flag and the anthem, idolized in victory, disgraced in defeat. The Olympiad has become war conducted by other means.

OMBUDSMAN, *n.* A person hired by governments or news organizations to deal with troublesome matters in such a manner as to justify what went wrong.

OMNIPRESENT, *adj.* To be in all places at the same time; said to be true of God as well as government, except when a policeman is needed.

OMNIVEROUS, *adj.* Capable of eating anything. One of the most appetizing descriptions of man is that he is herbiverous, carniverous and, above all, omniverous.

ONE-UP, *adj.* (colloquial) Having an advantage over another, which is all right, but not as good as being two- or three-up.

ONOMATOPOEIA, *n.* (Greek) If you have to look up the meaning of this word, it is clearly not what you are looking for.

OODLES, *n. pl.* (slang) A very large amount.

Oodles of noodles
Aren't very good
For people or poodles;
Oodles of anything

Aren't very good
For peasant or King;
Unless the oodles
Are oodles of gold,
Then they are good
For any old thing.

SMOOT SWISH

OPEN-FACED, *adj.* A frank, honest sandwich, which is hard to find these days.

OPEN-MINDED, *adj.* What each side in an argument wants the other to be, i.e., empty-headed.

OPPORTUNITY, *n.* What America is the land of, if you've had the opportunity to know the right people at the opportune time.

ORGY, *n.* An occasion of wild, mindless merrymaking, like the office Christmas party or a political convention.

OUTGOING, *adj.* Describing a friendly person about to be retired from office.

OUTLAW, *n.* An in-law with whom one is on the outs.

OUTSPOKEN, *adj.* Describing what a person will be if he or she dares to argue with a traffic policeman, judge, or politician.

OVERCOME, *v.* According to the song, what we will eventually do, if we are not long gone first.

OVERKILL, *n.* What the nuclear powers have achieved, based on the doctrine that if 1,000 nukes are good, 2,000 are better; the final manifestation of the self-destructive tendencies of mankind.

There's something comforting about overkill.
We gaze in awe at the technical skill

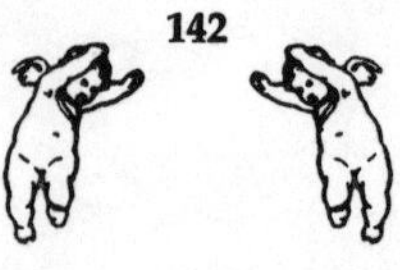

Ready to make the world all barren and still,
For when there's a way somebody will.

ATLAS K. MELTIN

OYSTERS, *n. pl.* Seductive marine mollusks that people fry, slurp, or stew—(and pretend to enjoy) under the mistaken belief that they will improve their sex life; a sort of culinary trade-off.

PACIFIST, *n.* A logical person who believes that since peace is so much better than war, it is not worth fighting for.

PAGEANT, *n.* An elaborate procession or display. There are two kinds: patriotic, which invoke duty, and pulchritudinous, which invoke beauty. The latter generally provides prettier scenery and draws more enthusiastic audiences.

PAIN, *n.* An unpleasant sensation; nature's way of signaling trouble, unless the pain is located in one special area, such as the neck, when it is more likely that a human is the culprit.

PAPER, *n.* The substance of which money, magazines, books, and newspapers are made, not to mention tigers. It also creates work, known as paperwork, to the delight of lawyers and bureaucrats and the despair of everyone else.

PARANOIA, *n.* 1. The erroneous belief that someone dangerous is following you, whereas we all know that it is the person ahead of you who is dangerous. 2. A favorite diagnosis of psychiatrists except in their own case.

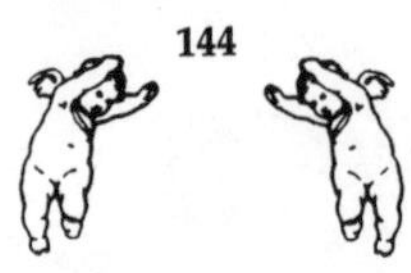

During the 1965 New York City blackout, a patient was visiting his psychiatrist. When the lights went out it was the psychiatrist, not the patient, who jumped up and shouted, "They're coming to get me." Perhaps it takes one to know one?

PARATROOPER, *n.* A brave and daring soldier who descends into a battle area or behind enemy lines with only a parachute for cover.

PARDON, *n.* The forgiveness one can ask of another without the assistance of a minister or a lawyer.

PARENTHOOD, *n.* A demanding occupation with long hours, low pay, little respect, few vacations, and no chance for promotion; a dead-end job, where you can't even refuse to do windows, and yet the number of applicants seems inexhaustible.

PARENTING, *n.* 1. A recent movement encouraged by experts who believe that old mistakes of child-rearing can be corrected by new ones. 2. A deplorable program in which parents, or people about to become so, are instructed in the right ways to bring up their children who, of course, are not consulted about the matter. One result of this dubious practice is that the children are inspired more to talk than to listen, which shows how bad habits are formed early in life.

PARIAHS, *n. pl.* Social outcasts, the latest examples of which are cigarette smokers, overweight people, terrorists, and similar depraved types.

PARKING LOT, *n.* A place that is always filled with a lot of cars by the time you arrive. A parking place is one that has already been taken.

PARKWAY, *n.* A place where cars are driven, as distinguished from a driveway where cars are parked.

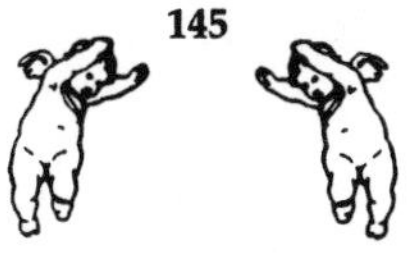

Take me out to the parkway,
Take me out for a drive;
Traffic may be a problem—
The roads are always alive—
But if we get home to the driveway
We can park and exchange a high-five.

TITUS TWICK

PARTICIPATING DEALERS, *n. pl.* The ones that can never be found when television commercials announce a special opportunity you are interested in.

PARTY, *n.* In contracts, the one of the first part who is always at odds with the one of the second part, which leads to a parting of the ways, known as breaking the contract.

PASSPORT, *n.* An official document entitling one to travel internationally at his or her own risk, as long as he or she possesses Visa cards.

PATRIOTISM, *n.* A smoldering nationalistic sentiment, evoked by governments when appeals to greed and glory have been exhausted.

PATRONAGE, *n.* Political jobs or favors. This is particularly important in democracies because without it, the winners could not be distinguished from the losers in elections.

PAY AS YOU GO, *adj.* A commendable financial practice, not honored by the United States government which prefers a practice of don't pay as you go broke.

PAY TV, *n.* A system in which viewers pay directly for the programs they watch without the interference of commercials; as distinguished from commercial television, which is paid for by commercials and thus regarded as "free" to the viewers, regardless of the psychic harm and higher prices those commercials produce.

PEACE, *n.* A period of time long enough to create the conditions of, and make the preparations for, the next war; but brief enough to prevent people from becoming accustomed to it. If the latter were to occur, peace might be preferable to war, which would be dangerous to foreign policy.

PEARLS, *n. pl.* Those infrequently found gems which constitute the main justification for the existence of oysters.

PECUNIARY, *adj.* Having to do with money (which is valuable) and why peculation (the act of embezzling) is one of the least peculiar peccadillos of peccable (sinful) man.

PEDAGOGUE, *n.* A pedantic synonym for teacher, but with a better connotation than demagogue which bears some resemblance.

PEDESTAL, *n.* A place upon which idolized objects are set. Since women, as well as men, have fallen, only pets remain.

PEEKABOO, *n.* Formerly a childish game, now an adult game played with garments.

PENTAGON, *n.* 1. The military headquarters of the U. S. Department of Defense, an organization of high officials, technicians, and bureaucrats more concerned with defending their budgets and pensions than with defending the nation. 2. A quaintly designed building, so massive and complex that in any given period of time more visitors are lost in its corridors than in combat; they are classified as "Pentagone." 3. The hot-house of interservice rivalry. 4. A word that has become synonymous with all that is stupid and wasteful in big government.

PERFUNCTORY, *adj.* Mechanical or indifferent, taking its name from the way functionaries perform their duties.

PERIOD, *n.* The preferred way of ending a sentence if it is written rather than ordered by a judge.

147

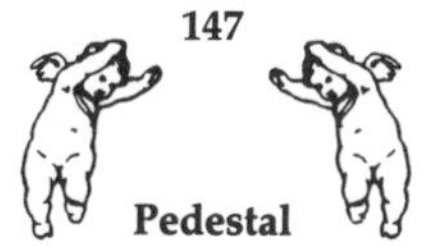

Pedestal

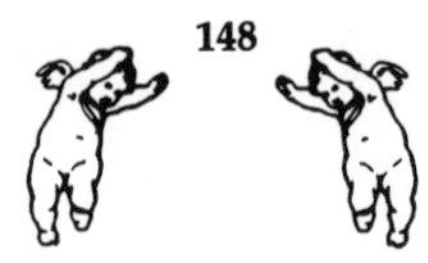

PERJURY, *n.* The serious offense of lying while under oath. Fortunately, people are not often under oath, therefore not loath to lie everywhere else.

PERMANENT, *adj.* A provisional extension of the temporary. It is a paradox of life that most things deemed permanent tend to become temporary, e.g., marriages, while the things deemed temporary tend to become permanent, e.g., the "temporary" inconvenience of urban construction or road repairs.

PERSECUTION, *n.* An evil form of harassment, lacking the legality of prosecution or the finality of execution.

PERSISTENCE, *n.* Perseverance that has taken a turn for the worst.

PERSONALITY, *n.* A social grace which some people have more of than others, the latter preferring to have character.

PERSPECTIVE, *n.* The thing that all troublesome matters must be properly placed in, to the advantage of the one doing the placing. The most important aspect of a perspective is that it be "meaningful." (See MEANINGFUL.)

PERSPIRATION, *n.* What sweat is called in the high-rent district.

PERTINENT, *adj.* Being relevant and to the point. It easily becomes impertinent, however, if pursued too far, especially by juniors.

PESSIMISM, *n.* An admirable attitude with which to confront the folly of optimism in a world of realism.

PETS, *n. pl.* Favorite animals, treated with love and affection. If children are the last, best hope of mankind, then pets are the last, best hope of children.

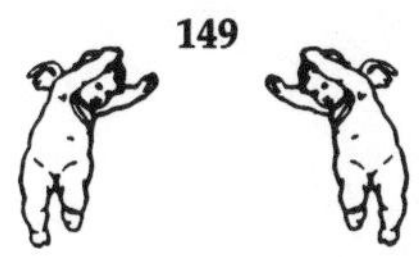

PHARMACOLOGY, *n.* The science of drugs, which has attracted the attention of athletes, entertainers, and other seekers after truth.

PHI BETA KAPPA An honorary society, members of which receive a key as a symbol of their lock on academic erudition.

PHILANTHROPIC FOUNDATIONS, *n. pl.* Benevolent institutions whose executives find it so difficult to give money away wisely that they wisely follow the old adage of beginning charity at home.

PHILOSOPHY, *n.* The profound attempt to discover the meaning of life, by one who thinks more about it than lives it.

PHOTOGRAPHS, *n. pl.* Pictures taken to please the family, bore the neighbors, and enrich the camera shops.

PICARESQUE, *adj.* Dealing with rogues and their adventures, examples of which are *Moll Flanders,* political memoirs, and *The Congressional Record.*

PICTURES, *n. pl.* One of these is said to be worth a thousand words, assuming that it is in focus.

PITY, *n.* A soft sentiment, comforting to express, but without much redeeming value.

Pity the avid poker player
Lacking a needed ace, or
The young and anxious lawyer
Trying to win a case.

Pity old Judge Crater
Gone without a trace, or
Troops advancing forward
Without a rear-guard base.

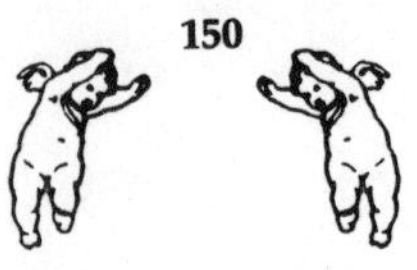

Pity the pious Anglican
Risking a fall from grace, or
The earnest Oriental
Concerned with losing face.

Pity the reckless American
Who has to win the race, or
The team of Russian athletes
Ending in second place.

Yes, pity all of these
As time proceeds apace,
But pity most the cosmos:
Man has reached its outer space.

IPWOT SPRUNK

PLAGIARISM, *n.* The academic, and probably illegal, sin of knowingly using someone else's ideas, writings, etc., as one's own without proper acknowledgment or permission. This is almost impossible to avoid completely. The late historian, Carl Becker, wrote somewhere that if one stole from a single source it was plagiarism, if from twenty sources it was scholarship.

PLATFORM, *n.* The shaky collection of fabricated planks that political parties stand or run on at their peril. As is usual with theatrical events, more attention is paid to the performers than to the platform upon which they perform.

PLATONIC LOVE, *n.* A deep, but nonerotic, affection between a man and a woman, said to be play for one and tonic for the other.

PLEASURE, *n.* Enjoyment or delight; a goal of everyone, but brought to the peak of perfection by what Veblen might have called (but didn't) "the pleisure class."

PLUMBER, *n.* An expensive artisan who keeps the spigots flowing, the toilets flushing, and the drains running on time.

PLUNGE, *v.* What the stock market thoughtfully does on one day so that it can soar on another.

PLUTOCRACY, *n.* A government in which the rich rule—as if there were any other kind.

POLICE ACTION, *n.* A modern way of describing a war that no one had the courage to declare.

POLICE BRUTALITY, *n.* The deplorable, excessive use of force in stressful situations by enforcers of the law. Contrary to the claims of the Benevolent Order of Police Officers, it does occur, primarily because cops are not ordinarily recruited from devotees of tea parties and croquet matches; neither are thugs. It also occurs when peaceful demonstrators demonstrate an excessive zeal for peace by throwing molotov cocktails, or insist that looting, starting fires, and shooting firearms are harmless exercises in civil rights.

POLICY, *n.* 1. The incomprehensible document issued by insurance companies in return for premiums that provide more profits than protection. 2. A very elastic term that can be stretched to include plans, practices, procedures, goals, hopes, beliefs, and aspirations—which is why it is impossible for anyone to explain either a foreign or domestic policy to the satisfaction of others.

POLITICAL PARTIES, *n. pl.* Organizations of citizens more interested in winning elections than in providing good government since to the spoils belong the victors. In the United States there are three political parties: the first, the second, and the third. The first, alphabetically, is the Democratic Party, consisting of liberals and progressives. The second is the Republican Party, consisting of conservatives and right-wing extremists. The Third Party consists of moderates, liberal conservatives, and conservative progressives; it gets its name from the fact that it always finishes third in elections.

POLITICAL SCIENCE, *n.* The purported science of government. It has contributed as much knowledge to that arcane subject as astrology did to astronomy, phrenology did to psychology, and alchemy did to chemistry. In the modern world, it is more likely that the politics of science has much greater significance than the science of politics.

POLITICAL SOLUTION, *n.* In international affairs, the one that is rightly sought in preference to military solutions, even if it means merely postponing the inevitable explosion to a later date. It buys time, if not always peace.

POLITICS, *n. pl.* In public affairs, the games that are played in scheming for power. Politics has been referred to as the "art of compromise," but if so there is a heavy accent on the last two syllables.

POLLS, *n. pl.* Formerly, official locations where, at designated times, votes were officially cast and counted. Now, they are conducted officiously (but not officially) at any time, anywhere, by people called pollsters who have become the oracles and arbiters of our time. People used to go to the polls; now the polls and pollsters come to them. Impertinent in conception, and pernicious in consequence, they demean *Vox Populi* into *Pox Populi.*

POLYGRAPH, *n.* A lie detector. Originally and intuitively perfected by parents, spouses, and lovers, it has since been botched up by scientists who invented a machine that cannot distinguish between lying, crying, or trying.

PORK BARREL, *n.* (slang) The bottomless container of public funds used by legislators to bring home the bacon to their constituents.

PORNOGRAPHY, *n.* 1. The purported erotic stimuli emitted by a pornograph, which may be in the form of a photograph, a paragraph, or a phonograph. 2. A close relative of obscenity, in that both terms belong to a legal family that is rapidly dying out.

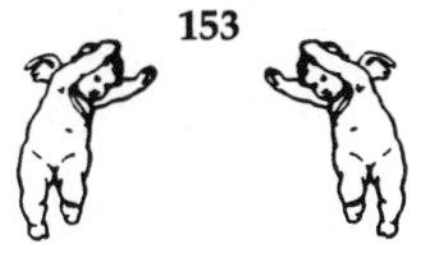

POSTERITY, *n.* Generations of the future, about which more concern is expressed than the future of generations, which is dubious.

POSTULATE, *v.* To take for granted or assume without proof. Like the man who was surprised to learn that he had been speaking prose all his life, people postulate more than they think.

POT HOLES, *n. pl.* The stuff of which streets and highways are made; government's indirect way of subsidizing tire dealers and the automobile repair business.

POWER, *n.* The capacity to control people and events, requiring a steady diet of it, regular exercise of it, and no sleep if it is to be retained—as many uneasy heads learned. Power is much easier to lose than to acquire.

Power:
Once it's been gained,
It can't be contained,
And the fruits it obtained
Soon vanish with the
Flower.
Unused to using it,
Prone to abusing it,
The penalty is losing it:
Such a brief, lonesome
Hour.

HIRAM WHIPPLE

PRACTICAL JOKER, *n.* A person in danger of needing a practical nurse.

PRAGMATISM, *n.* A doctrine in which the value and truth of ideas are tested by their practical consequences rather than impractical wisdom. The question, "practical to whom or for what purpose?" is not part of pragmatic discourse, since the answer is assumed to be self-evident.

PRAYER, *n.* An earnest request for divine assistance or guidance. It may be silent or spoken, with equal probability of desired results.

PRECEDENT, *n.* In law, the decision in an earlier case used to justify the desired verdict in a present case. Precedents are drawn upon when they support the conclusion already reached, or ignored when troublesome. Many more precedents are established than are followed, which is why so many court decisions are unprecedented.

PREDESTINATION, *n.* The comforting doctrine that one's ultimate destination was determined even before the journey began. It saves the trouble of consulting maps and travel agencies.

PREOCCUPATION, *n.* Something that commands all of one's attention, as distinguished from occupation, which only requires some of one's attention occasionally.

PRESIDENT, *n.* In the United States, a person who endures a number of primary grades, graduates from a conventional high school, works his way through the Electoral College, finally graduating with an advanced degree of fatigue and a temporary job.

PRESSURE, *n.* A term invented by sportscasters to describe what athletes are under in tense moments of competition. Should the pressure be felt in the throat, it is known as "choking," which provokes utmost disgust among those not involved. The extent to which athletes actually experience the heavy pressure often attributed to them is debatable. Bill Lee, a rather droll major league pitcher, was once asked how much pressure he felt on the mound. "Thirty-two pounds per square inch at sea level," he replied.

PREVENTIVE WAR, *n.* The somewhat muddled doctrine that it is better to prevent a future war, which may or may not take place, by making sure that one takes place now.

PRICE CUTTING, *n.* A lowering of prices by one competitor against another, in the effort to gain more customers. Since this practice also happens to benefit consumers, it is universally despised in business circles as a form of treason.

PRIDE, *n.* A high opinion of one's own worth, merited or not; a fragile thing, easily hurt or injured. It can be either a notable deficiency of character, known as vanity and conceit, or a conspicuous ingredient of gallantry and determination—usually the former—whence it goeth before a fall and after a promotion.

PRIMARY, *adj.* That which is placed ahead of what is secondary.

PRINCIPLE, *n.* The thing it is always a matter of when a person's actions are more absurd than usual.

PRIORITIES, *n. pl.* The ordering of alternatives in terms of importance, while failing to specify the criteria used. To establish priorities accomplishes two things: it impresses others that some thought has apparently been given to the matters at hand, and it permits one to deal with the first item of the hidden agenda in a seemingly rational way.

PRIVATE, *adj.* Away from the public, or not public. Privacy is not a right protected by the Constitution, hence as fragile as it is precious. It is a curious law of civilization that private affairs become more and more public knowledge, through the media and the courts; and public affairs become more and more private, through secret deals, closed committee meetings, and the traditional smoke-filled rooms.

PROFESSIONAL, *adj., n.* Formerly, a term reserved for the learned occupations, such as law, medicine, or teaching. Now, the meaning has been expanded to include, among others, the professional politician, soldier, informer, criminal, i.e., simply a way of life. The ultimate usage will be a "professional professional."

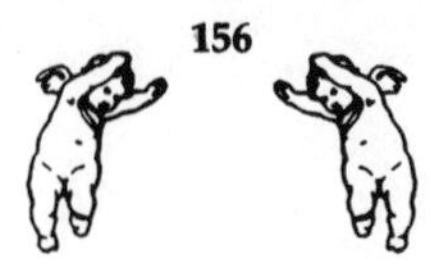

PROFESSOR, *n.* A teacher of the highest rank in a college or university. A person who has spent his or her life sharing ignorance with, and learning from the wisdom of, students.

PROGNOSIS, *n.* A guess as to what is likely to happen, as distinguished from a diagnosis, which is a guess as to what *is* happening.

PROGRESS, *n.* The long, slow ascent of man from simple, primitive savagery and barbarism to complex, sophisticated savagery and barbarism.

PRONE, *adj.* Either to be prostrate, or be inclined to. Cleopatra is reputed to have captured its full meaning when she said to Mark Antony, "I am not prone to argue."

PROPAGANDA, *n.* What education is called if it's on behalf of an unpopular cause.

PROPOSAL, *n.* An offer of marriage, which is several advances above a proposition.

PROPRIETY, *n.* Conventional standards of proper behavior, located somewhere between property and piety, and sharing the smug virtues of both.

PROSECUTION, *n.* Persecution, when it is conducted legally by the state.

PROSTITUTION, *n.* The world's second oldest profession, the first being that of procurer.

PROTESTANTS, *n. pl.* Any of various tribes of Christians who prefer to hide their sins rather than confess them.

PRUDE, *n.* A person who is imprudently criticized for being prudent in matters prurient.

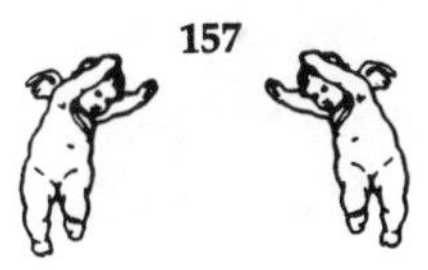

PSYCHIATRISTS, *n. pl.* Rich cousins of psychologists; both devote their lives to probing the mysteries of human psyches—a practice which tells more about their own psyches than those of their patients.

PSYCHOANALYST, *n.* Another prober of the human psyche, reputed to go down deeper, stay down longer, and come up dirtier than the non-Freudian psychiatrist.

PUBERTY, *n.* A time of life when the loins stir and the brain loafs. Later the processes are typically reversed.

PUBLIC GOOD, *n.* An important social and political value, helped most by people who neither talk about it nor work at it.

PURGATORY, *n.* A condition of temporary suffering known as parenthood.

PUTS, *n. pl.* The things that are constantly being lost during the ins and outs of daily life. ("It is my observation that in Washington, and elsewhere, there are far more inputs than there are outputs. This means that a large number of puts are disappearing somewhere in the process. God knows where they'll eventually turn up."—Edwin Newman, *A Civil Tongue.*)

PUBLIC OPINION POLL, *n.* An ingenious statistical device that lifts something called "opinions" off the top of a few heads, flies them through a mass of hot air, called "demographics," and finally lands them at an influential airport called "public opinion."

QUACK, *n.* (slang) A person who dishonestly pretends to be a physician, as distinguished from an M.D. who honestly pretends to be one.

QUADRISYLLABIC, *adj.* An extravagant word, requiring five syllables to describe a four-syllable word; a good example of how language becomes both more complex and more incomprehensible.

QUAINT, *adj.* Describing anything amusingly strange or odd, such as calling a tax increase "revenue enhancement."

QUAKER, *n.* A member of a Christian group known as the Society of Friends, which remains that way by holding meetings thoughtfully characterized by extensive silence.

QUALIFIED, *adj.* Possessing the proper qualities or skills for a particular job or occupation. This permits applicants to be politely rejected on grounds of being over-qualified, i.e., a possible threat to the one doing the hiring.

QUALITATIVE, *adj.* Concerned with quality, values, or

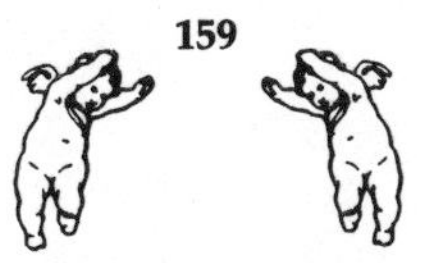

merit, as contrasted with quantitative, which is concerned with quantity or numbers. When the two are in conflict, the latter can generally be counted on to win.

QUALMS, *n. pl.* Feelings of doubt or misgiving, such as those suffered when taking an oath, signing legal documents, or making New Year's resolutions.

QUANTUM JUMP, *n.* In physics, the same as a quantum leap, so long as they both obey the principle of uncertainty.

QUARK, *n.* One of the six paired fundamental particles of the universe. Two are known as top and bottom, the other four being in and out, and up and down. Sadly, only one is known as charming.

Hark! Hark! The Splendid Quark
Dwelling there in Particle Park;
It comes in sixes, not in sevens,
But lucky yet for earth and heavens:
It didn't come in sad elevens.
Still, I find it quite alarming,
Puzzling, odd, and disarming,
That only one is cute and charming.

QUINTUS QUIRK

QUARRELS, *n. pl.* Angry disputes that are prevented from becoming feuds if all the disputants have no living relatives. The things that keep families, neighborhoods, and nations alert.

QUARTER, *n.* 1. What one should not give when hard-pressed. 2. A heavy drinker.

QUESTIONABLE, *adj.* Doubtful or uncertain, which is what the answers to most questions unquestionably are.

QUOTATION, *n.* An apt phrase or statement, never recalled until it is too late to be useful, and then attributed to the wrong source.

R, *n.* If your child is exposed to three of them in school, you are fortunate indeed.

RABBIT'S FOOT, *n.* A token of good luck to the hare-brained.

RACE, *n.* 1. A foolish concept, the most profound meaning of which is a group of people engaged in a running contest. 2. An historical absurdity that has been used to justify such noble doctrines as Aryanism, the White Man's Burden, the Yellow Peril, Black Power, and White Supremacy. The only significant race is the human one, and it's in enough trouble without adding colorful doctrines.

RACISM, *n.* 1. A subject of modern doctrinal dispute between Good and Evil. Good racism asserts that racial groups exist, but are inconsequential. Evil racism asserts that racial groups not only exist but are of overriding importance. Both sides agree that either form is moral and legitimate if invoked for a greater cause. 2. A troublesome doctrine to everyone except those who know how to exploit it to their own advantage.

RADICAL, *n.* An extremist in political, social, and economic affairs. A radical of the left seeks rapid, fundamental change in one direction; a radical of the right seeks the same in the opposite direction. Both lack a reliable compass, but are extremely sure of their bearings.

RADIO, *n.* A means of communication, now used primarily to bring country-western music to eastern, urban populations in exchange for the privilege of hearing rock 'n roll.

RADIOASTRONOMY, *n.* The means by which we will receive messages from intelligent life in outer space—if they were sent millions of light years ago in English or some other ancient language.

RAGE, *n.* Violent anger. When kept within, it is destructive, but when directed outward, as outrage against some vicious stupidity, it is not only constructive, but ennobling. The capacity to be outraged is a mark of honor.

RAINBOW, *n.* A spectrum of colors that appears in the sky when, on occasion, rain and sun and clouds collaborate to produce another of nature's works of art.

RAISE, *v.*, *n.* 1. What parents do with children if they do not neglect the rearing of them. 2. A pay raise is one that lifts you into a higher tax bracket and a lower standard of living.

RANK AND FILE, *n.* A felicitous way of describing members of an organization. Those with rank have privileges, those in the file have duties. The former rankle the latter, while the latter foil the former as much as possible.

RAP, *n.* (slang) Either what one beats, or takes, depending upon the skill of the lawyer or the size of the bribe.

RAPTURE, *n.* The very great joy one is occasionally filled with, such as when deliberately missing several acts of a

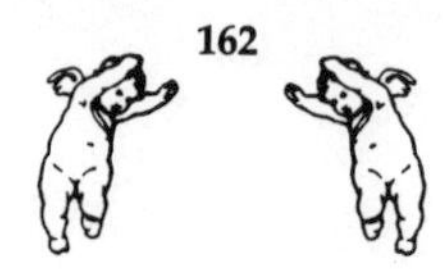

Wagnerian opera, or evading an invitation to another dreary reception.

RARA AVIS, *n.* (Latin) A person or thing seldom seen or met, even if you try harder.

RATIONAL, *adj.* The type of thinking that appeals to our prejudices without unduly straining our credulity.

REACTIONARY, *n.* In politics, an extreme conservative who prefers to react to events rather than act to bring them about—and, when possible, to do neither.

REAGANOMICS, *n.* A controversial doctrine of the 1980s which proclaimed that when the Ship of State, with a crew called Reaganauts, rescued (that is, stole) the Golden Fleece, it be divided among the crew rather than distributed to the spectators.

REALIST, *n.* A person for whom things poetic or imaginative have no meaning; one who would locate the Land of Oz on a map, and "September Song" on a calendar.

REALLY, *adv.* A word which, together with y'know, constitutes the basis of a modern vocabulary: "Really . . . y' know," "y' know . . . really," and so on.

REAPPORTIONMENT, *n.* The questionable way the political party in power brings the voters of congressional districts to their census.

REASON, *n.* An excuse, offered as an explanation. Be cautious of anything that stands to reason: it may not be self-supporting.

RECALL, *n.* The attempt to remove someone from public office by popular vote. It succeeds if enough voters recall the evils that prompted the attempt in the first place. Those who are not recalled should not be forgotten.

RED-BLOODED AMERICAN, *n.* One more interested in the statute of limitations than the Statue of Liberty.

REFORMER, *n.* A zealous person who claims to know not only what is wrong with the system but how to put it aright. One who has the tendency to fix what is not broken, and to break that which is whole. This is why the reforms of one generation breed the next generation of reformers, since further repairs are always necessary.

REGRESS, *v.* To move backward, as opposed to progress, which means to move forward. Both imply a sure sense of direction, which is conspicuously absent.

REGULATION, *n.* An innocent-sounding synonym for coercion.

REMEDY, *n.* In medicine, a generally recognized cure for a generally recognized disease; in law, a vague prescription for an uncertain ill.

REPARATIONS, *n. pl.* The compensation extracted by the victors from the losers in one war to finance preparations for the next one.

REPORTEDLY, *adv.* A vague but indispensable word in modern journalism. It is used to include such diverse sources as, "A cab driver told me on the way to the office"; or "I think I read it somewhere"; or "It really hasn't been reported, but there's been talk about it."

REPRESENTATIVE, *n.* A member of the lower house of Congress, as distinguished from a Senator, who is a member of the upper chamber. Sceptics believe nothing is lower than either.

REPRESSION, *n.* A neologism used to fine-tune the economy when it is somewhere between a recession and a depression. A linguistic trick to hide bad news.

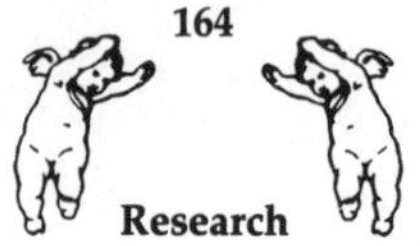

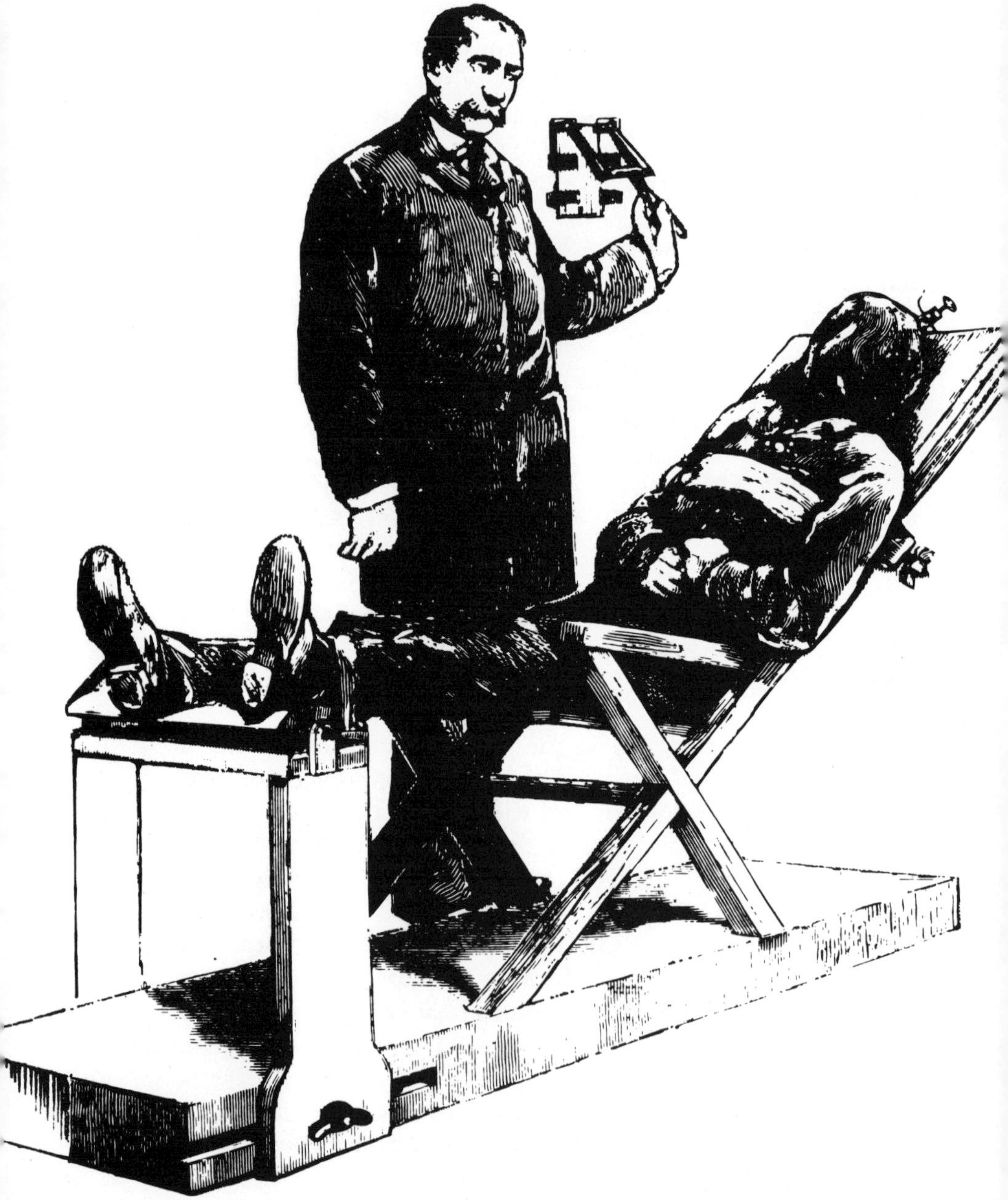

REPUBLICAN PARTY, *n.* A political organization that began with the Great Emancipator and has retreated to the Great Communicator.

RESEARCH, *v.* Literally, to search again or search anew, i.e., another search to demonstrate that the original search was erroneous, and the reason why further research is always needed.

The brightest words in all of science,
The ones that have succeeded,
Are those that end the papers:
"More research is needed."
Research means funds and projects,
Basic, pure, applied;
"More research is needed"
Is the call to which it's tied.
Yes, "More research is needed,"
And so 'twill always be,
As long as frontiers beckon
And the funds are there to see.

FLAVIUS FLAGON

RESORT, *n.* A place to visit for fun and relaxation. The last resort is one where relatives plan to be.

RESPECTABILITY, *n.* The social status of people whose sins haven't quite caught up with them.

RESPONSIBILITY, *n.* A burden people are willing to assume in order to blame others for things they were not responsible for.

RETINUE, *n.* The group of attendants and sycophants, without whose presence no celebrity would be complete.

RETIREMENT, *n.* A time in life when people who are tired from work are entitled to become tired from other activities. (As the statistician said: "Here we are, broken down by age, sex, and occupation.")

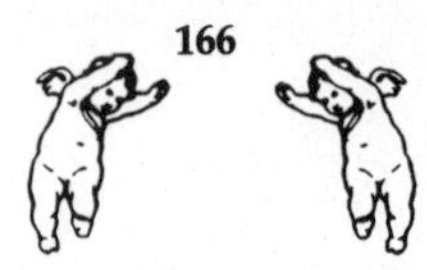

REVOLUTIONARY MOVEMENT, *n.* A political upheaval that begins in the brain of a visionary, flows to the hearts of the faithful, and thence to the bowels of the mob.

RICH, *adj.* The condition of having more money and property than most people, less than is desired, and not enough to satisfy the Internal Revenue Service.

RISIBILITY, *n.* The precious capacity to laugh, even at ourselves—what Oscar Wilde might have called (but didn't), "The Importance Of Not Being Earnest."

ROCK 'N ROLL, *n.* 1. A primitive form of music, played by savages for the edification of barbarians. 2. A grossly unpleasant way of acquiring deafness at an early age.

ROMANTIC, *adj.* Describing a form of love based so much on sentimentality that the sentiment overwhelms the mentality.

ROOKIES, *n. pl.* Inexperienced persons, especially in the first year of professional sports. In baseball, it is the time to learn how to spit; in basketball, to foul; and in football, to slug, without being caught.

ROOMMATE, *n.* Formerly, a person of the same sex with whom one shared a room; now a person of either sex, with more emphasis on the mating than the rooming.

RUDE, *adj.* Discourteous and impolite—one of the first things children learn to be by imitating adults.

RUG, *n.* A convenient covering for sweeping unpleasant things under, until the time arrives to pull it from under the unsuspecting.

RUSSIA, *n.* The Soviet Union—a nation of many languages that speaks with one tongue.

SACRED, *adj.* Holy, worthy of reverence and awe; a variant spelling of scared.

SACRED COW, *n.* Anything that has been baptized, anointed, and sanctified by the popular media which can, by the same token, consign it to the hell of oblivion.

SACRIFICE, *v.* To give up something valued for the sake of a higher good—what everyone wants someone else to do for its ennobling contribution to character-building.

SADNESS, *n.* An agreeable emotion, bringing much private happiness so long as there are witnesses to its display.

SAGACIOUS, *adj.* Wise, astute; a compliment given to those whose judgments resemble our own.

SALT, *n.* The acronym for Strategic Arms Limitation Talks, which everyone seems to be taking with a grain of.

SANITY, *n.* Good mental health, a condition difficult to identify in a world of such rampant insanity. How is it to be determined, and by whom, when psychiatrists themselves are suspect, and juries are not particularly noted for their collective rationality?

> There is a story—probably apocryphal, but told by a former Senator—of a man who had once been hospitalized with a mental breakdown, then was certified to be sane and released. He insisted that his "clearance" be written. Later he was elected to the Senate of the United States, where he claimed to be the only member who could now prove he wasn't crazy.

SATIRE, *n.* A delicate form of humor, demanding straight thinking, cut on a bias.

SAUNA, *n.* A potent steam bath, very popular with the wealthy and powerful as a means of sweating out their crimes and sins.

SCANDAL, *n.* An unsavory episode, made so only by the fact that what was once private is now public. The participants are shamed by the righteous, whose own sins have not yet been exposed.

SCHOLAR, *n.* 1. A person who received so much education, little was left over for the rest of us. 2. One who has exploited the scholarly works of others so artfully as to merit promotion and tenure. See PLAGIARISM.

SCHOOL, *n.* An educational establishment where teachers decline to teach for fear of losing their jobs, and students decline to learn for fear of losing their friends.

School days, School days,
Good old fun 'n fool days:
We offer them our praise.
The teachers didn't teach,
No learning did we reach,
As each was true to each.

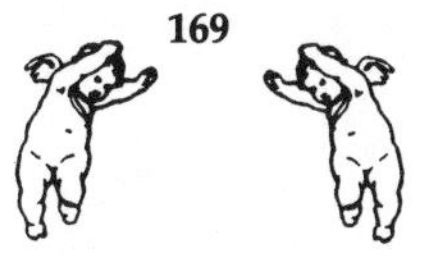

For as the memories recede,
We see the experts have agreed:
Schooling's not for education,
Just a thing for graduation,
And the cause for celebration.

LIONEL GRUMP

SCHOOL YEAR, *n.* A long, painful period of time consisting of twenty months for students, thirty for teachers.

SCIENCE, *n.* A form of exact knowledge, that is produced by people called scientists (blessed is that tribe), using a method called scientific (holy of holies), thereby causing many theological disputes as to what is known and not known and by whom.

SCORES, *n. pl.* Good things to keep, the better to settle.

SEASONAL ADJUSTMENT, *n.* 1. A mysterious operation performed on most important statistical reports, such as unemployment rate, retail sales, etc., to make them conform to the average climate for that time of year. 2. During the baseball season, a statistical correction for hits and errors; during the football season, for yards gained and lost.

SECRETARY, *n.* An invaluable person who remembers what the boss forgets, and forgets what no one should remember.

SECULAR, *adj.* The same as the sacred, after the collection plate has been counted.

SECURITY CLEARANCE, *n.* What one must obtain to have access to classified and sometimes important documents. From all reports, possession of a social security number and a bank account is sufficient for the purpose. Students of the matter have concluded that the biggest security risks are the people who do the classifying and the clearing.

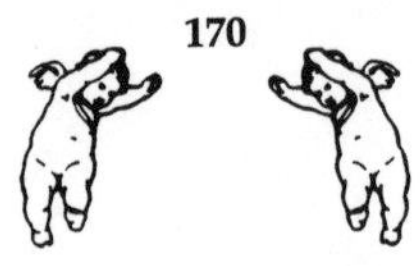

SEDITION, *n.* A crime committed by government, whose acts incite rebellion on the part of the people offended.

SELECT COMMITTEE, *n.* A small group of legislators, appointed to investigate a particular incident or problem, so carefully selected that the proper outcome is assured.

SELF-DISCOVERY, *n.* The voyage of life, severely hampered by conflicting navigational aids, the appearance of unexpected storms, and numerous collisions with other selves lost in the same sea.

SELF-RESPECT, *n.* The pride that cannot be self-conferred; it must be delivered by others who are in the same trouble.

SELF-RIGHTEOUSNESS, *n.* Self-respect corrupted by conceit.

SEMI-CIRCULAR, *adj.* Describing a type of reasoning that has not run its full course.

SEMPER FIDELIS, Latin) Always faithful, the famous motto of the U.S. Marine Corps, having the great virtue of being noncommittal about the object of faith.

SENIOR CITIZENS, *n. pl.* The appallingly witless appellation given, in a fit of morbidity, to elderly people—presumably because they are about to graduate, not from college but from life.

SENTIMENTALITY, *n.* Excessive feelings of tenderness, promoting the sentiment, and demoting the mentality.

SERMON, *n.* A long-winded way of saying "Thou shalt not."

SERVICES, *n. pl.* A vital part of the total economy of goods and services, which is why the economy is in such bad shape: the services aren't good, and the goods aren't serviceable.

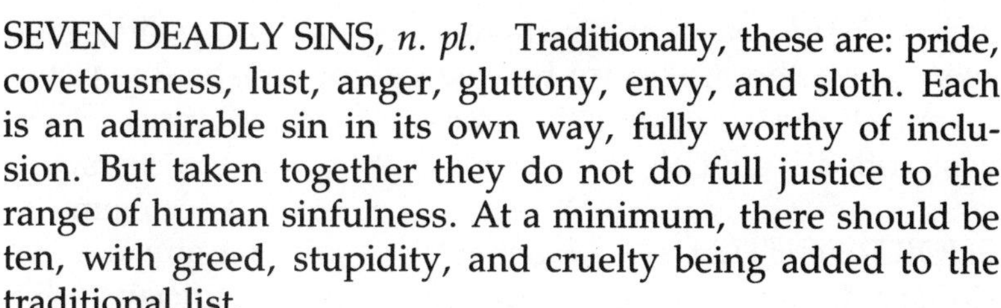

SEVEN DEADLY SINS, *n. pl.* Traditionally, these are: pride, covetousness, lust, anger, gluttony, envy, and sloth. Each is an admirable sin in its own way, fully worthy of inclusion. But taken together they do not do full justice to the range of human sinfulness. At a minimum, there should be ten, with greed, stupidity, and cruelty being added to the traditional list.

SEXUAL HARASSMENT, *n.* A reprehensible act that occurs when, in the war between the sexes, the male advances and the female retreats; or vice versa.

SEXUALITY, *n.* One of the most startling revelations of the twentieth century. Previously unknown, or unrecognized, it was discovered accidentally on a rainy day when two feminists and a gay clinical psychologist were cleaning out a closet. Ever since, sexuality has become the subject of a widespread search, since it may be found lurking in places other than closets.

SHAKESPEARE, *n.* Either the person who wrote the immortal literary works attributed to him, or another person entirely; or another person with the same name.

SHAKY, *adj.* Weak, not firm, like many an agreement made with a handshake.

SHOCKING, *adj.* Appalling, outrageous, a quality hard to find anymore. Most moralists now think that with the rise of modern sophistication, the shock market has crashed beyond salvation.

SHOGUN, *n.* The title of the chief military leader of traditional Japan, as well as the title of a very popular novel and television mini-series (which was scarcely minimal in length); also useful for robbing a Japanese bank.

SHOOTING WAR, *n.* A hot one, where military weapons are used, as contrasted with a cold war, which lacks the firepower.

SHORTFALL, *n.* In the rhetoric of modern politics and economics, the difference between an optimistic forecast of revenues and an optimistic forecast of expenditures, otherwise called a deficit.

SHORT-SIGHTED, *adj.* Unable to see very far ahead. A visionary disease of business executives and politicians who, respectively, think the next quarterly report and the next election exhaust the future.

SHORT STORY, *n.* A possible novel, cut down to size.

SHOW, *n.* A performance that must go on, as required by tradition, often going on much too long for the comfort of spectators.

> Adlai Stevenson once told an audience: "I am here to speak and you are here to listen. If you should finish before I do, please don't hesitate to leave."

SHRINK, *n.* (colloquial) A futile term with which to belittle a psychiatrist.

SIBLING RIVALRY, *n.* The competition between two or more children in the same family for the scarce resource of parental affection and attention. In a one-child family, this is replaced by parental rivalry, of which not too much is spoken.

SIGNAL, *n.* The hidden true meaning of a diplomatic communication as divined by suspicious diplomats unused to plain talk.

SIGN LANGUAGE, *n.* In its modern form, billboards.

SILENCE, *n.* The golden voice of discretion to which everyone should listen more often, especially when arguing.

SIN, *n.* Wrongdoing, or breaking divine law—always more obvious among persons who are disliked anyway for other shortcomings.

SITTER, *n.* A very important addition to the modern family.

SKIM, *v.* To remove from the top, or to read carelessly; the former is more profitable in Las Vegas, the latter in Washington, D.C.

SLUMS, *n. pl.* The poorest, dirtiest, most crowded parts of a city that produce some neat and tidy sums for landlords.

SMALL, *adj.* Describing the chance of success of a large reduction in the federal deficit, and the minds of the people quibbling over it.

SMATTERING, *n.* Slight knowledge; what most people have of most things but don't realize it. Oscar Levant did when he titled his book *A Smattering of Ignorance.*

SMELL, *v.* To sense with the nose, which means that nosy people may smell more, but without more sense.

SMOKE SIGNAL, *n.* Among some American Indians, a very important means of communication conducted by covering and uncovering a fire.

> It has been reported that when the first atomic blast rose over the Los Alamos desert, it was observed by some neighboring Indians. As the mushroom cloud ascended, one Indian said to the other, "I wish I'd said that." It is doubtful if anyone would say that now.

SMOKISM, *n.* This new word is not yet to be found in standard dictionaries. It is a logical extension of all the derogatory "ism" language currently fashionable: elitism, racism, sexism, ageism, etc. It is the belief that people who smoke tobacco, especially cigarettes, are vile, depraved scoundrels and sinners, despoiling the environment and carelessly injuring the health of everyone. Being inferior, smokers should be treated as such, segregated from decent folk, and made to suffer the indignities appropriate to their status. A smokist is one who practices this doctrine and attempts to incorporate it into law.

SNEAK ATTACK, *n.* A surprise assault by an enemy before war has been properly declared. This is roundly condemned in military and diplomatic circles, not because it is unfair (what *is* unfair in war?), but because the enemy not only thought of it first, they also successfully executed it.

SOAK, *v.* What tax plans may attempt to do to the rich, when the usual sources of revenue have run dry.

SOCIOLOGY, *n.* A social science that generates great quantities of trivial studies presented in impenetrable language of shallow profundity. The following specimen taken from a public document may not be fully representative, but is not entirely atypical either.

> The initial phase of Data Analysis involves the development or modification of special analytical methodologies. These can include trip hierarchy modeling, computerized flow simulations and data-oriented network restructurings. Methodologies . . . will be employed wherever possible to facility (sic) input/output compatibility.
>
> During the analysis phase, interactive processes that explore all possible data orchestrations, projective simulations utilizing a full range of feasible scenarios, programmed walk techniques, and structured zoning will enable the development of quantitative parameters for a

real world master plan for public transportation . . .

SOLITAIRE, *n.* A popular card game played by one person. It has the unique advantage that the only one who can be cheated is the one doing the cheating.

SOUL, *n.* Energy or power of mind and spirit.

Breathes there a man with soul so dead,
Who ne'er to himself has said:
"I wonder what she's like in bed."

RICKY RUMPLE

SOUL SEARCHING, *n.* The dangerous self-examination of one's motives, beliefs, etc. It is dangerous because of the tendency to be satisfied with finding the wrong flaws.

SOURCE, *n.* The point of origin of many news stories, variously identified only as being informed, well-placed, knowledgeable, reliable, authoritative, etc. The thing they have in common is anonymity, and an anonymous source has no more standing in the court of credibility than an anonymous accuser has in a court of law.

SPACE AGE, *n.* What the current period of history is often called because of the construction and launching, at enormous expense, of thousands of gadgets into outer space. Time used to be money; now space is. The timely question of this age is how much time is left to enjoy or benefit from this conquest of space.

SPITBALL, *n.* A technically illegal pitch in baseball that has polished off many a legal game.

SPY, *n.* One of a secret army, hired to obtain secrets without giving away any.

Ellsworth Eden was quite a guy,
For his country he became a spy.

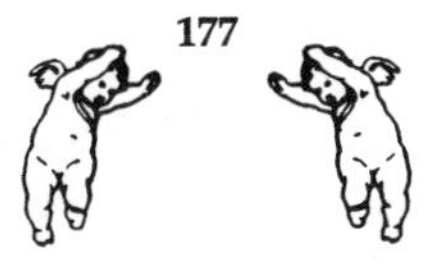

With belted coat and glasses dark
He thought it just another lark
When passing signals in the park
Or watching dogs that never barked.
But other countries had their spies
Their informers in disguise,
Finding secrets, telling lies,
And Ellsworth Eden wasn't wise.
Someone talked and blew his cover,
Someone's friend, someone's lover;
So, one night, asleep in bed
The trap was sprung and he was dead:
Should have quit while still ahead.

Roscoe P. Slooth

SQUANDER, *v.* To spend foolishly; waste. All top officials in the Pentagon must first pass a test in the art and science of squandering, after which a security clearance is automatic.

STATE, *n.* A political and geographical unit of the United States that has few rights left.

STATESMAN, *n.* An elderly politician who has survived his errors and his enemies, and been forgiven for both.

> As President of the United States, Mr. Herbert Hoover became a symbol for everything evil and inhumane. For years he was publicly reviled and scorned. Time passed, circumstances changed, and in the last decades of his life he became an admired man. On his ninetieth birthday, now hailed as an elder statesman, he was asked about his new reputation. "I outlived the bastards," he explained.

STATISTICS, *n. pl.* The collection, analysis, and interpretation of numerical data in such a way as to be understood by computers and misunderstood by everyone else.

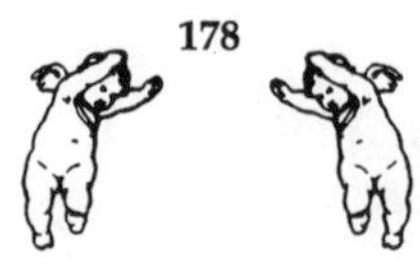

STEALTHY, *adj.* Done in a secret manner; the way politicians steal in order to become wealthy.

STEREOTYPE, *n.* A conventionally negative image of some group or category of people, in which individual diversities are hidden under a falsely attributed uniformity. An elementary way of creating prejudices.

STICKING POINT, *n.* An issue that brings negotiations to a halt, i.e., when no one will stick up for any talking points.

STICK TOGETHER, *v.* To be united and support each other; what people vow to do only when no other alternative is available.

STONE, *n.* An object which, if one casts it first, is likely to be returned with interest.

STONEWALL, *adj., v.* (slang) A nickname that made a Civil War general famous, and a practice that made a civilian President infamous.

STOUT, *adj.* What one should be of heart, not of girth.

STRANGE, *adj.* Unusual or peculiar. The reason that truth is stranger than fiction is because it is so unusual to hear it.

STRANGER, *n.* A person who lives next door or across the hall.

STRATEGY, *n.* 1. The grand design of a war, conceived far from the scene of action, as distinguished from the attack-tics, which is where the casualties occur. 2. What wars are lost or won in spite of, not because of.

STREETS, *n. pl.* The arteries of modern cities, clogged with traffic, pitted by pot holes, prowled by criminals, and generally dangerous to health and welfare.

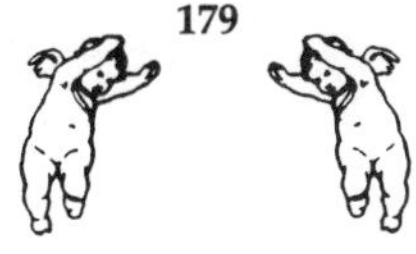

STUFFED SHIRT, *n.* (slang) A below-the-neck version of a swelled head.

STYLE, *n.* The characteristic way a person disguises lack of substance, and therefore is looked upon with respect and admiration in the world of politics and television.

SUBORN, *v.* To cause witnesses to give false testimony in court, so they may redeem themselves by being suborned again.

SUBSIDIZE, *v.* To aid or assist with money, which has become the major domestic activity of the federal government. Everything from business to farming to education profits from a federal subsidy of one kind or another. One of many absurdities is highlighted by the spectacle of Congress and the Surgeon General warning everyone about the health hazards of smoking cigarettes, while tobacco production continues to be subsidized under political pressure.

Sentinel: Halt. Who goes there?
Smoker: Just another smoker, sir.
Sentinel: Advance smoker and be recognized
For exactly what you are:
Another person who is scorning
The General's righteous warning
About that nicotine and tar
You will cough across the bar.
Who do you think you are?
Smoker: Sir, I am just a humble man
Who doesn't live by national plan
Or join every caravan.
The General is a prudent man
And I admire his public stand
Against the weed I hold in hand;
But even with his deep concern
There are some things I wish to learn.
Sentinel: Speak up, you smoking man;
I'll tell you what I can.

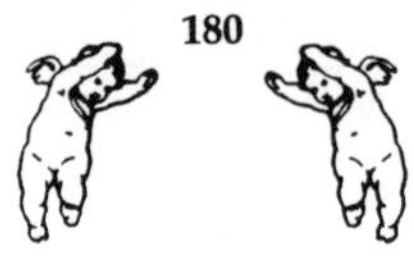

Smoker: I know it's not my place to ask
But neither can I wear a mask.
If what the General says is true,
That cigarettes should be taboo,
Are not there other things to do?
Perhaps he could prepare reports
To end tobacco price supports.

Sentinel: Surely, you must recognize
That the General has his ties
To a Congress very wise;
Tobacco farmers have a lobby
While your smoking's just a hobby.
Any group that's organized
Must by law be subsidized,
Even though it's realized
That other goals are jeopardized.
To deny tobacco its support
Would be an act of last resort,
Like closing down some useless fort
Or bringing mobsters to a court.

Smoker: But if the General is so committed
Why are cigarettes permitted?
Isn't there some legal force
To solve the problem at its source?

Sentinel: Even you must realize
We can't prevent free enterprise
From making things a person buys:
With one strong hand we subsidize
And with the weaker criticize.
That's the democratic way
To make the total system pay.
Of course we wish to guard your health
But not in ways that threaten wealth:
Taxes, jobs, and dividends,
Like profits too, are noble ends.

Smoker: Now I begin to understand
Why cigarettes cannot be banned,
And why a warning must suffice
To everyone who has the vice:

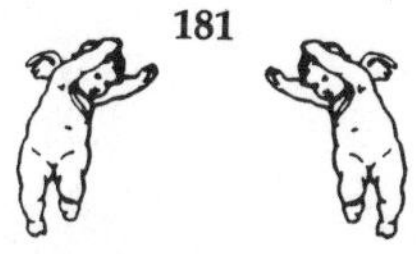

Beyond the cost, there is a price,
And reason's froze as if in ice.

PETER PACKER

SUBURBS, *n. pl.* Residential areas near cities where the residents have reached a certain station in life: railroad for commuting, wagon for shopping.

SUCCESS, *n.* That uncertain point in a person's life when it is more rewarding to look back than ahead.

> Some years ago a retired Shakespearean actor opened a confectionary shop. As he had learned and maintained the baking arts of the Old Country, the quality of his products was unmatched; but customers were few. One day alone in the shop, he noticed how drab the bare walls looked. That evening he purchased reproductions of some paintings he had always liked and had them framed. When they were hung in the shop, he was pleased, for they added much color, charm, and warmth.
>
> Soon his few regular customers noticed the additions and they, too, were pleased. They told their friends, who then became customers, and told their friends. Rapidly the little business thrived beyond all hopes, and it seemed as if the customers came as much to enjoy the art as to enjoy the pastries. The successful mix of art, aromas, and confections made the owner both proud and grateful.
>
> To express his appreciation in proper theatrical form, each night as he closed the store, he would gaze at his handiwork and murmur softly, "Good night, sweet prints, I'll sing to flights of angels for the sweet smell of thy success."

SUFFRAGE, *n.* In democracies, the precious right or privilege of voting, earned by suffering through all the pains of election campaigns.

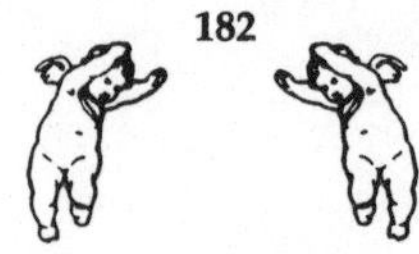

SUMMITRY, *n.* A telegenic game played by heads of state to a worldwide audience, with full knowledge that no one will come out on top.

SUPER, *adj.* Informally designating anything deemed excellent or superior; what was once an adolescent word of praise has now been appropriated for anything and everything, much to the detriment of language.

I don't know about you
But I'm in something of a stupor
About the increasingly deplorable view
That almost anything merits being called "Super."

Of course, I want to emphasize
That not for a moment would I wish to curb
The use of superlative or supervise,
Superintendent, superstition, and surely not superb.
It seemed quite natural in supernatural
And supercilious didn't make me bilious.

But superbowl, supermarket, and superstar
Are misplaced and decidedly inferior.
Super city, block, or superette are clearly not superior.

Enough is more than enough, methinks;
This usage is painful; it stinks.
And when I hear of a superduper blooper
I return again to my super stupor.

(With apologies to Ogden Nash,
who is not responsible.)

SUPREME COURT, *n.* A judicial body consisting of five consenting, and four dissenting, adults of various legal persuasions.

SURGEON, *n.* A gifted person, born with an ice cube in the heart and a golden scalpel in the hand.

SYMMETRY, *n.* A graveyard with a British accent.

TABLE TALK, *n.* Conversation at meals. In business, it consists of triple martinis, double crosses, and single checks. In the family, it disappears with the onset of adolescence or the purchase of a television set.

TABOO, *n.* A strong ban or prohibition, often sacred in nature, such as forbidding meals made from humans, or telling your lawyer the truth about what really happened. "Taboo or not taboo" is a question that has vexed anthropologists since the time of Shakespeare.

TACITURN, *adj.* Describing a person not fond of talking, a quality most people appreciate because it gives them that many more turns to talk.

TACT, *n.* The art of handling an awkward situation gracefully, as distinguished from diplomacy, which attempts the same but requires lying as well.

> An old hand in the hotel business explained the difference to a newcomer as follows: "If you are on room service and mistakenly enter a room

Tango

while a lady is dressing, and you say 'Excuse me,' and shut the door behind you, that's tact. If, under the same circumstances, you say 'Pardon me, sir,' and continue to enter the room, that's diplomacy."

TAKE-HOME PAY, *n.* The expendable income remaining after all the expandable deductions have been extracted.

TALES, *n. pl.* Stories about more or less interesting events; the most interesting are those told out of school.

TALION, *n.* The principle of making the punishment fit the crime; an eye for an eye, a tooth for a tooth, or three congressmen for a senator.

TALKING POINT, *n.* Something to use in an argument or negotiations, especially useful when blunt language is not possible.

TANGO, *n.* What it takes two to do, when one is not enough and three is too many.

TANGIBLE ASSETS, *n. pl.* Material possessions, as opposed to the other kind, which are not only intangible, but also immaterial.

TANKER, *n.* A huge ship that carries oil, despoiling many ports and beaches along the way.

TAX ACCOUNTANT, *n.* An honorable person who, for hire, will honestly aid you to the best of his ability in the nonpayment of taxes.

TAXES, *n. pl.* In one of his famous decisions, Mr. Justice Holmes wrote that "Taxes are what we pay for civilized society," by which he seemed to mean bad laws, bad roads, and a lot of red tape.

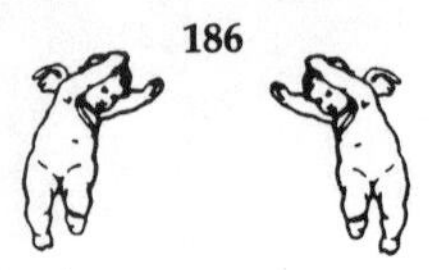

A former Director of the Bureau of Internal Revenue, Mr. Mortimer Caplan, had the last, best word when he was quoted by *Time* as saying: "There is one difference between a tax collector and a taxidermist—the taxidermist leaves the hide."

TEACHER, *n.* A person who gets paid for transmitting ignorance to the young, as distinguished from parents, who must pay for the privilege.

TECHNICAL, *adj.* Treated in a highly specialized, disciplined manner, so as to confuse the non-specialist, and often to cover the specialist's ignorance. When, for example, a change in the stock market is called a "technical adjustment," it means the speaker doesn't know what in the hell was going on. Similarly, when someone says, "In a technical sense . . ." you can be sure that some meaningless nonsense will follow.

TECHNICALITY, *n.* Some trivial point, or detail, that courts seek in trials to make sure the law is properly upheld and the litigants are improperly held up by attorneys.

TEENAGER, *n.* A sixteen-year-old, going on thirteen.

TELEVISION, *n.* A monstrous mode of mass communication, geared to the lowest common denominator on Main Street, and the highest common stock on Wall Street, the former producing the latter. Television is a continuing race to see which network can out-copy the others, for the programs have a monotonous similarity of mediocrity. As Fred Allen once remarked, "Imitation is the sincerest form of television."

TEMPORARY, *adj.* Lasting only a relatively short time. Fortunately, most things *are* temporary, permitting us to endure them in good humor, and with the comforting thought that "This, too, shall pass."

TEMPTATION, *n.* That which can be resisted only in one's Wildest dreams.

TERRORISM, *n.* The ancient practice of violence that has shocked the modern conscience—not because of the violence, which is commonplace; and not because civilians are injured or held hostage, for that, too, is commonplace—but because terrorists do not follow the usual rules of war. Further, modern terrorists have learned how to use television as an extraordinary weapon, with the connivance of the news media, against which there is no known defense.

TESTING, *n.* A mania of our times; a contagious disease of the mind that is spread by gullibility, and a belief that testers know best. There is no known cure.

TEXTBOOK, *n.* One that introduces students to an accumulation of known errors in such a way that they will be perpetuated without being questioned.

THEISM, *n.* Belief in one God, the one who has acquired at least a temporary monopoly in the marketplace of religion.

THERAPIST, *n.* In psychology, an infernal meddler with an advanced degree of some kind, and usually licensed by the state, thus giving him or her greater license to ruin the lives of others while enriching their own.

THICK-SKINNED, *adj.* Not sensitive to criticism, a quality most notably associated with thick-headed people.

THINK TANK, *n.* (colloquial) A place where a number of intellectuals are assembled to cogitate over the profound issues of the day. This assures results even more bizarre than could possibly have been achieved by each separately.

TOASTMASTER, *n.* A person who presides over a dinner, primarily to tell jokes and introduce the speakers. One genial toastmaster confided that he could make a good living at bull fights since he had so much practice at opening the door for the bull.

TOLERATE, *v.* To endure what is disagreeable or disgusting without visible signs of anguish. This is heralded as a virtue, especially in an age of permissiveness. We are urged to tolerate the intolerant and the intolerable in the name of tolerance, which is more than can be endured.

TOME, *n.* A certain kind of book, admired more for its size, weight, and thickness than for its content and readability.

TONGUE, *n.* The movable fleshy organ in the mouth, used for tasting and talking. This is a most convenient arrangement when it is remembered that good taste prevents a lot of bad talk.

TRANSPLANT, *n.* A modern surgical miracle whereby someone's diseased organ can be replaced by a healthy organ from another person, or even animal, under the right circumstances. Through the medium of television, transplants threaten to become a new medical industry. Not many patients can be helped thereby, but the surrounding publicity creates instant heroes for an audience in dire need of them and of miracles.

TREE OF KNOWLEDGE, *n.* In Biblical terms, recognition of good and evil. Apparently, the tree was chopped down, or uprooted, in the Garden of Eden and never replanted. At least, its whereabouts have never been discovered despite all the searching of generations of philosophers and theologians.

TRICK OR TREAT, *n.* A playful Halloween practice, whereby children are taught the art of extortion, i.e., that threats are amusing ways to achieve being well-treated.

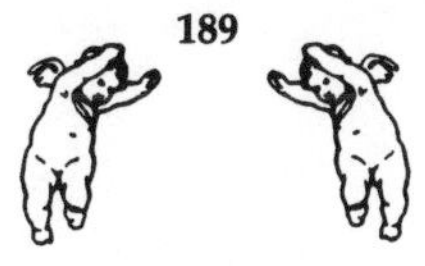

TRIGGER-HAPPY, *adj.* A good way of becoming trigger-sorry.

TRILOGY, *n.* An interminable way of making three novels do the work of one.

TRIP, *n.* Just what is needed to spoil a vacation.

TRIVIA, *n. pl.* Things of little or no importance. A preoccupation of the modern mind, to which large, important matters have become either unthinkable, unbearable, or both. Trivia replace news, are the subject of discourse, and components of popular books and games. Mastery of trivia is the current sign of learning.

TRUISM, *n.* A half-truth which, like the Big Lie, has been repeated so often without question that its truth is beyond dispute.

TUNNEL, *n.* An artful contrivance through which to see the light at its end; often used by generals and journalists as a passage to optimism.

TURPITUDE, *n.* Wickedness, usually moral, i.e., sexual, in character, thereby absolving political or industrial wickedness from the same stigma. The latter sins are merely "infractions."

TWEEDLEDUM AND TWEEDLEDEE, *n.* What two useless things are called when they are nearly identical; the names of the two-party system in the United States.

TWENTIETH CENTURY, *n.* A 100-year period that went from the 19th century to the 21st without growing up. Beginning in the age of innocence, it had an adolescent spurt in science and technology, but not in wisdom. It suffered a mid-life crisis, called World War II and the Atomic Bomb,

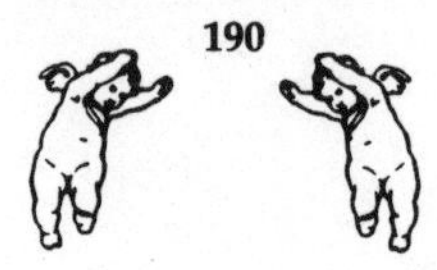

from which it never recovered, reaching a terminal stage before its time.

TWIST, *v.* To distort the purpose and meaning of words; a fine art as practiced by lawyers, political opponents, and other experts in distortion.

TYPO, *n.* (slang) A Freudian slip committed by a neurotic typewriter.

> Freud himself reported on an Austrian journalist who referred to a famous general as being a "bottle-scarred veteran." When this slur was indignantly protested, the journalist made amends. In the correction he admitted his error, and wrote that he intended to say "battle-scared" veteran.

TYRANNY, *n.* The arbitrary or excessive use of power, which all governments practice as both a right and a duty; they differ only in the amount of velvet in the glove, if there is a glove at all.

ULYSSES, *n.* A remarkable novel originally made famous by its unintelligibility and alleged obscenity; then made even more notable by the fact that no one knows what James Joyce wanted the final text of this masterpiece to contain.

UMPIRE, *n.* In baseball, an authority figure who calls balls and strikes at his own whim.

> Three umpires were discussing their work. One said, "When the pitch comes in and the ball is over the plate, it's a strike." Another said, "When the pitch comes in and the ball misses the plate, it's a ball." The third said, more accurately, "When the pitch comes in, that ball isn't anything until I say what it is."

UNALIENABLE, *adj.* The rights which, according to the Declaration of Independence, include life, liberty, and the pursuit of happiness—so long as these don't interfere with needs and goals of the state.

UNBLINKING, *adj.* What the visual stance of a person or nation should be when going eyeball to eyeball with an-

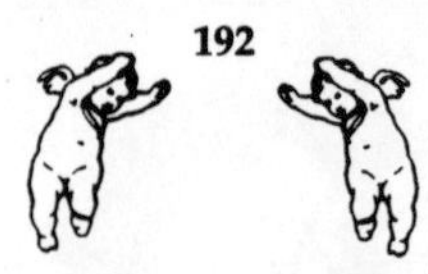

other—which is rather silly, if not unsightly. Presumably, one should also not sneeze if going nose to nose with someone, which is impossible to avoid if going eyeball to eyeball.

UNCONSCIONABLE, *adj.* Describing an act that offends the conscience of the one doing the describing.

UNITED FRONT, *n.* The specious claim of unity made by bitterly hostile groups who, at least temporarily, have more to fear from outsiders than from each other.

UNITED NATIONS, *n.* A legally established international entity, with a charter and everything, including lavishly ornate headquarters in New York City. Its initials, U.N., are often thought to stand for Unable Nations. Known more for its opulent life-style than for its authority or effectiveness, it is addicted to passing resolutions when not otherwise engaged in abstaining, vetoing, or spying. It is also disproportionately subsidized by the United States, a nation despised and opposed by most of its members, which testifies again to our national wisdom.

UNITED STATES, *n.* 1. A nation whose condition is serious but not hopeless, in contrast to the United Nations whose condition is helpless but not serious. 2. A nation-state, republican in form, democratic in process, and anarchist in spirit.

UPRIGHT, *adj.* A term that more accurately describes human posture than probity.

URBANE, *adj.* Courteous, refined, elegant; formerly thought to be characteristic of urban populations, this demeanor has deteriorated to the point of being suburbane.

URBAN TRANSPORTATION, *n.* Sick Transit Uproaria.

VANITY, *n.* Excessive pride in looks, ability, or accomplishments; deplorable when revealed by others, but regarded as poise and self-confidence in ourselves.

VATICAN, *n.* The Pentagon of the Church militant, and the Wall Street of the Church secular.

VAUDEVILLE, *n.* A form of entertainment that featured song and dance teams, bad jokes, and trained animal acts. It was pronounced dead about the same time the antics of Congress became more publicized and appreciated as a similar form of entertainment.

VENTRILOQUISM, *n.* The art of making sounds seem to come from another mouth; now in evidence principally through speech writers, cue-cards, and teleprompters.

VERSATILITY, *n.* The commendable ability to do many things well—a capacity to which increased specialization is averse, if not hostile.

VERSION, *n.* A particular account of an event. There are

two kinds: the official version, and the correct one, of which more is known of the former than the latter.

VESTED INTEREST, *n.* A group that resists change for fear of losing its shirt.

VIABLE, *adj.* Capable of life. This is another word so frequently abused that, hopefully, it will be put to rest along with meaningful and interface.

VICE PRESIDENT, *n.* In the United States, a person with a better than average chance for future misery.

Vice Presidents have little to do
But sit and wait, and wait and sit;
John Garner said the job wasn't
Worth a bucket of warm spit.
(The quote was altered just a bit.)

The V.P. attends state funerals
(For the Chief he will pinch-hit),
And if the Senate has a tie vote,
He'll be there to break it.

Now, we wonder when it will be
That the V.P. is known as she.

ROCKFORD BUSHBY

VICTIM, *n.* A person injured or damaged or dead because of a crime; the "forgotten man" (and woman) of the criminal justice system.

VICTORY, *n.* The illusion of success in battles, and the delusion of supremacy in war.

VINDICATE, *n.* To clear from suspicion or charges of wrongdoing. This may be possible in a legal sense, but not in a social sense, for the seeds of suspicion sprout quickly, spread rapidly, and penetrate too deeply to be overcome by a few grains of truth later on.

VIRILITY, *n.* Manly strength and vigor, displayed less for the admiration of women than for gratification of the self.

VISIBLE, *adj.* Capable of being seen, or readily evident, and thus misleading. It is much easier to observe the face and body, which are visible, than the brain and heart, which are not.

VISITATION, *n.* The act of a friendly visit, or a severe affliction. The former becomes the latter more frequently than is realized.

VITA, *n.* (Latin) An exaggerated account of one's accomplishments.

V-J DAY, *n.* The holiday celebrating the defeat of Japan in World War II and the resulting victory of Japanese industry and exports.

VOCATION, *n.* Formerly, a word meaning an occupation or type of work; now, only a single letter separates it from both vacation and avocation, a fine line indeed.

VOICE, *n.* What democratic peoples want to have in their government, so long as it carries no responsibility.

VOLUNTARY COMPLIANCE, *n.* A vaunted claim of the United States tax system, which thoughtfully reminds citizens of their willingness to pay taxes by such reinforcements as mandatory withholding of portions of wages and salaries, the forced payment of estimated taxes by those whose taxes are not withheld, the threat of audits, and an assortment of mysterious regulations and penalties not fully comprehended by anyone.

VOODOO, *n.* A body of beliefs and practices that includes sorcery, magic, economics, statistics, and other forms of superstition.

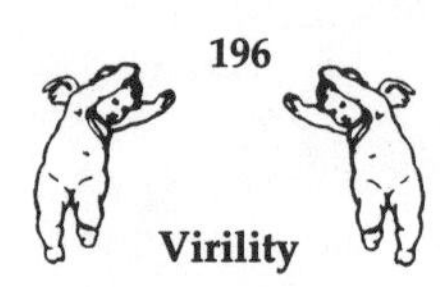

196

Virility

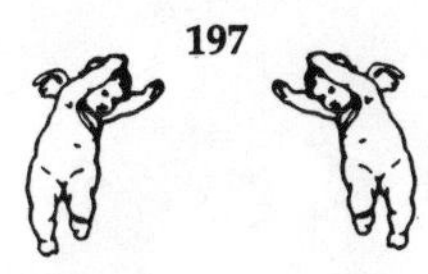

VORACIOUS, *adj.* Greedy, unable to be satisfied—characteristic of insurance companies, public utilities, tax collectors, alumni associations, and campaign treasuries.

VOTING, *n.* A periodic democratic exercise that brings out the worst in people.

> In 1984, during the frenzy of all the presidential primaries, an experienced foreign diplomat observed, "After watching your political campaign madness, I have become a born-again monarchist."

VOW, *n.* A solemn promise, usually extracted from a reluctant person under grave conditions of stress and duress.

VULGARITY, *n.* Bad taste, or coarseness of expression—what is required in a literary blockbuster, a box-office smash, and a high TV rating.

WAIST, *n.* A part of the human body that expands at the same time one's clothes shrink.

WAIT-AND-SEE, *adj.* An unavoidable attitude on the part of anyone concerned about the future, except for those who prefer to see-and-wait.

WALL, *n.* The strong barrier between church and state, except when the nation is in trouble—then the Almighty suddenly becomes an old friend. This is well illustrated when, as is reported, the Chaplain of the United States Senate opens each session by saying, "The Senate of the United States is now in session. God bless the United States."

WAR, *n.* An age-old, universal, barbaric pastime that has now become civilized to the extent of establishing "rules of war," and "war criminals"—both of which are determined by the latest victors.

WARRANTY, *n.* A much-publicized guarantee of some sort, generally qualified by the adjective "limited"—which means that the small print should be read at least twice.

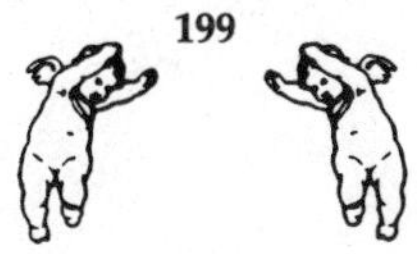

WASHINGTON, D.C., *n.* The capital city of the United States. A place where second- and third-rate minds grapple unsuccessfully with problems of the first order.

WASPS, *n. pl.* White Anglo-Saxon Protestants, a species that has lost its sting.

WATERGATE, *n.* A notorious political scandal that pulled a President of the United States down and investigative reporting up.

WATER HAZARD, *n.* What almost every lake, pond, well, river and reservoir now constitutes, with the generous assistance of pesticides, pollutants, acid rain, etc.

WEALTH, *n.* A highly valued possession that can be acquired by one of three means: birth, marriage, and luck, of which the last is most significant since it embraces the other two as well as being independent of them. Work is not included since it produces no wealth, but income only, and not much of that after taxes.

WEEK, *n.* A unit of time consisting of seven days and seven nights. No matter how it begins it always comes to a weak-end.

WELFARE STATE, *n.* An ingenious set of modern governmental programs designed more to protect the welfare of the state than to advance the state of general welfare. It fares well at the polls.

WHISPERING CAMPAIGN, *n.* What political opponents initiate when the usual amount of shouting seems ineffective.

WHITE HOUSE, *n.* A famous residence best known for having a spokesman, a switchboard, a rose garden, an oval office, and two temporary occupants.

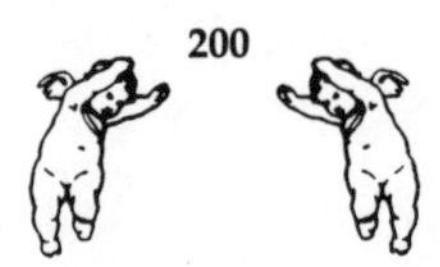

WHITEWASH, *n.* The fluid preferred over ink in preparing reports of investigative committees.

WICKED, *adj.* Bad, sinful; what Warren G. Harding would have called "normalcy." A person who burns the candle at both ends is said to be double wicked.

WILDERNESS, *n.* A barren place, where voices of doom are always crying to ears that won't listen.

WINE, *n.* An alcoholic beverage, imbibed for the sake of piety in church, and for the sake of insobriety elsewhere.

WINK, *n.* A deliberate movement of an eyelid to signal something better left unsaid.

WIRETAPPING, *n.* What various law enforcement agencies do with each other, for each other, or against each other—depending on what's on tap.

WISDOM, *n.* Knowledge and judgment acquired by experience, and disregarded by the inexperienced, insuring that the same mistakes will be repeated.

WITCH DOCTOR, *n.* The question a patient asks after receiving a second, conflicting opinion. It is also the answer.

WITHIN LIVING MEMORY. A perfectly innocuous phrase until one considers the alternative.

WORLD SERIES, *n.* In baseball, the supreme international sporting event of the year, sometimes involving teams from two adjoining countries—which shows just how small the world has become.

WRITER, *n.* A person dumb enough to sit at a typewriter; bright enough to roll sheets of paper into the machine; skilled enough to strike most of the right keys most of the time;

201

Wine

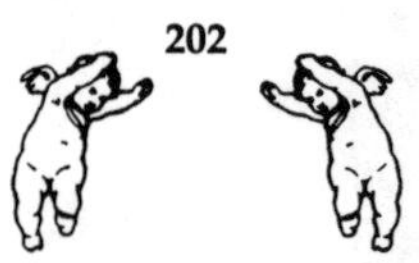

strong enough to look at a blank sheet of paper without weakening; stubborn enough to replace spoiled sheets with fresh ones; honest enough to be dissatisfied with what is written; vain enough to offer the result to an audience; and human enough to not take kindly to criticism.

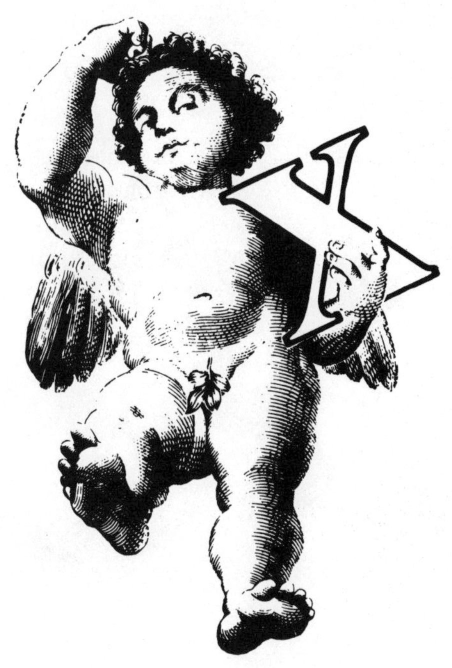

X-RATED, *adj.* The motion picture equivalent of a dirty book or magazine. If history is any guide, the X-rated film of today will be the G-rated film of tomorrow.

X, *n.* This letter is said to mark the spot that Johnny should be on.

XI The Roman numeral for eleven. Oddly, if you add the Roman numeral V, for five, you get fourteen instead of sixteen.

X-RAY, *v.*, *n.* An instrument used to reveal things that are otherwise hidden. Lungs are x-rayed in hospitals, luggage in airports.

YANKEE, *n.* A native of New England or a member of a New York baseball team. The former is famous for boiled dinners, the latter for getting boiled.

YES, *adv.* A word that has gotten many more people into much more trouble than the word "no."

YARD, *n.* The small area around a house that expands to infinity when it's time to cut the grass or rake the leaves.

YEARBOOK, *n.* One that every high school and college must produce annually as evidence that *something* happened.

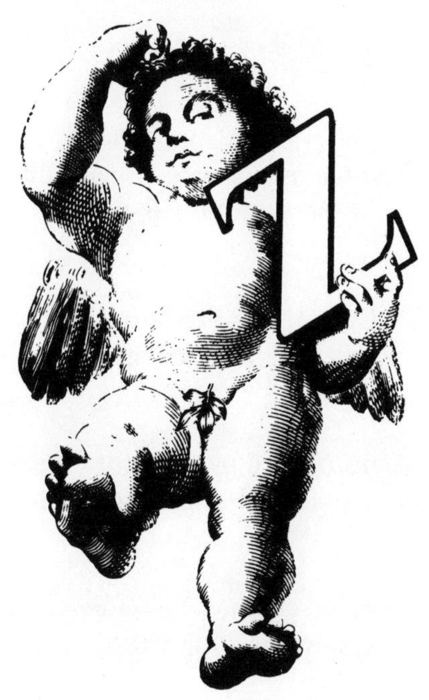

ZEAL, *n.* The necessary condition for becoming a zealot, which is remarkably close to being an idiot.

ZEITGEIST, *n.* A German word meaning the spirit or temper of the times, which is why so remarkably few good spirits or tempers are to be found.

ZERO, *n.* The absolute total meaning of all the words and worries that have been expended on a nuclear holocaust. If it happens, it happens, and the epitaph of the world will be, "From nothing to nothing, from Zero to Zero."

We were not present
When the world began,
But we'll all be there
At the final end of man.

No one was there
At the world's early dawn,
But billions will be present
When everything is gone.

Yes billions will be present
With not a single hero,

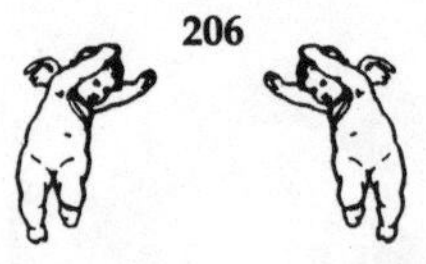

When the whimper turns to bang
And the final score is zero.

DIGBY DUMBLE

ZERO-SUM, *adj.* Describing the situation where a gain for one person *must* result in a loss for another, i.e., the typical social situation.

ZIP CODE, *n.* A numerical system introduced by the U.S. Postal Service to make sure that prompt delivery of mail will be further delayed.

ZIPPER, *n.* A metallic clothes fastener with the uncanny ability to know precisely the worst time not to work.

ZONING, *n.* An important ingredient of urban planning that thoughtfully divides cities into a number of combat zones to be fought over in the courts.

ZOO, *n.* A place where a variety of animals, birds, and reptiles are kept for public display. The most famous zoo is the Congress of the United States.